ALPHA FEMALES

Unleashed

from the
BOARDROOM

to the
BEDROOM

CC Lyons

Perfect Bound Edition
ISBN-13: 978-0-9989903-0-9

Electronic Edition
ISBN-13: 978-0-9989903-1-6

Library of Congress Number in Publication: 2017942080

HISPUBLISHING
GROUP
Division of Human Improvement Specialists, llc.

www.hispubg.com | info@hispubg.com

DEDICATION

This book is dedicated to the females of the past, present, and future, who are compelled to mask their unique "Alpha" being. Let it be known that you are not to mask it any longer. You are the epitome of power, beauty, and soul.

Thank you to those who seek to understand, encourage, support, and embrace the uniqueness of these powerful women.

Thank you to all of the men and women who participated in the research interviews in support of this book.

CONTENTS

FOREWORD

Finally, a great analysis and exposé is being unleashed on some powerful and talented beings (past and present). They have always been here: through the chronicles of history, in mythology, and via the oral traditions of many cultures, we have heard of their bravery, beauty, intelligence, strength, and strategic prowess. Most of history (or, "his story") has celebrated and reified the patriarch, as the triumphs and accomplishments of great Alpha men serve as both the foundation and the fabric of world history. In general, the great stories and valued contributions of Alpha Females have been episodic, exceptional, and secondary— often in support of their men and others.

In this bold and unprecedented deconstruction, CC Lyons takes a fresh and intriguing look at Alpha Females. The author takes us from the boardroom to the bedroom— offering a better understanding of their thoughts, their strategies, their fears and logic, while metaphorically walking in their shoes. Through this inside look into the mindset, motivations, and experiences of these powerful, independent, highly talented, gifted, and assertive women, we come to the realization that our labels of them as stubborn, aggressive, up-tight, callous, cold, and intolerable say far more about us, our insecurities, and biases, than it does about the capabilities, strengths, and accomplishments of these

1

powerful women. Maya Angelou's poem, "I Know Why the Caged Bird Sings," and Nina Simone's plea, "Please Don't Let Me Be Misunderstood," capture the fears and frustrations that many Alpha Females have endured in past and present society.

Fortunately, the dominant narrative is changing. Alpha Females have risen to positions of great power and stature in the present society and are featured prominently in television and movie roles. As an Alpha Male, I welcome and celebrate their increasing acceptance and prominence. They have always been a significant part of my life. I know them as mom, grandmother, aunt, cousin, daughter, friend, lover, colleague, role model, boss, mentor, advisor, and coach. I treasure my memories and experiences with them; their courage, vitality, wisdom, independence, nurturing, and support have largely shaped and developed me. My sincerest wish is that this book serves as a catalyst to a larger and needed dialogue about these powerful women and the role they can—and will—play in creating a better and more just society.

TWG

INTRODUCTION

*A*lpha Females Unleashed: From the Boardroom to the Bedroom exposes the "genetic mutation" of the Alpha Female. Instead of shunning her from the world, this book explains how to embrace and respect her, while harnessing all of the talents she possesses—for she cannot be tamed.

This is not a self-help book, nor is it intended to create a diagnosis. *Alpha Females Unleashed* will bring awareness of a particular type of female that has existed since the beginning of time. Its intent is to address myths and create dialog among all arenas of society in the acknowledgement and understanding of the highly considered taboo topic of the Alpha Female.

The food for thought this book provides looks to enable parents and family members to recognize her and encourage her; to give insight to the young Alpha Female as she matures in various areas of her life; to encourage corporate America to embrace her for who she is; and, for her suitors to understand her needs and moves and what it takes not only to capture her, but to sustain her.

This book gives "her" a voice, which others have tried to downplay or keep silent. The constraints are now removed and her voice is being unleashed.

CHAPTER ONE

The Mutant Revealed

Past, Present, and Future: She Exists

Imagine yourself stepping into a time machine, turning the dial back to get a "snapshot" glimpse of unique and game-changing women throughout history. What do you believe you would witness along that journey? Curious to know? Well, let the journey begin.

The first stop is to observe Eve charming Adam to defy God and eat the forbidden fruit from the Garden. She uses her intellect and seductive charm to convince Adam that eating the apple will do no harm and they will not be punished. How is it that she has that level of influence over him?

Fast forward to around year 51 B.C. to see Cleopatra become the Queen of Egypt. Four years later, she marries one of her brothers to ensure she maintains the throne; this, just one year after she takes Caesar as her lover. She has a son with Caesar, they move to Rome, and Caesar is assassinated one year later. She strategically, and with no emotion, has her brother killed to reclaim the throne; naming her four-year old son as the co-regent. Within that year, she seduces Mark Anthony, taking him as her lover. To satisfy her high libido, it is *rumored* that she fills a gourd with live, angry bees—creating the first female vibrator.

The next stop on the mythical journey peeks into Joan of Arc, who convinced the future ruler for France, Charles VII and his priest her divine mission was to save France during the Hundred Years' War. She dressed like a man to lead French troops to numerous victories *before* the age of 17. The English put her on trial for hearing the voices (she had the gift of hearing God), deemed her a witch and condemned her for dressing like a man. The English burned her at the stake in 1431 for her wartime accomplishments and powerful gifts. Later, France realized she was innocent and the Roman Catholic Church made her one of the few women Saints in 1920, St. Joan of Arc.

Next, watch Lucy Stone accept her diploma—being the first woman in Massachusetts to earn a college degree and organizing the first national women's rights convention.

Continuing the journey gains glimpses into the lives of Amelia Earhart—the first female aviator to fly solo across the Atlantic; the assignation of Indira Gandhi—the first (and only) female Indian Prime Minister; and the appointment of Sandra Day O'Connor as the first female Supreme Court Justice.

Fast-forward to brief images of Sally Ride and Mae Jemison entering into space as the first woman and first African-American woman, respectively, to accomplish this feat. Turn the corner to view 21st century women, Hillary

Clinton, first American First Lady to win a public office seat and to first woman in U.S. history to be the presidential nominee of a major political party; and Oprah Winfrey who—with a power known as the "Oprah Effect"—makes significant strides in politics, social influence, and international leverage.

Concluding the journey, you step out of the time machine into the present to view the story of Cantara, who is breaking the barriers of her culture and family tradition.

Cantara lives in the "po-dunk" country side of India. Much to the culture where the men are always seen as the dominant force of the family, Cantara plays with her friends, leading them in various activities. In her home, her father is very strict, dominating, and controlling to the point where she will not breathe hard around him, much less speak to him. At boarding school, she is the protector of her younger sibling. Her mother is stunned to learn that Cantara talks a lot and is perceived as "bossy" by the headmaster.

As Cantara matures, she excels in school and completes her undergraduate degree in her native country. The culture timeline dictates that once a degree is earned, marriage quickly follows. Marriage in her culture is not about two people—it is about two families. The parents play matchmaker to find mates for their children. One requirement is that the mate is from the same culture, cast, or status. Cantara, foreseeing the matchmaking routine, strategically decides to pursue her Master's degree in the United States. She knows she's not fit for the normal tradition and becomes determined not to be tied to it. A long-time male friend also decides to pursue his Master's degree in the United States.

The flight to the U.S. is Cantara's first plane ride. She is afraid to be so far away from home, surrounded by people that do not look like her, and unsure of the future. She starts to cry, but then compartmentalizes the fear by keeping her focus on the main goals of gaining her degree and finding a husband of her choosing. Her parents know and approve of her first goal; but not the second.

During her advanced-degree journey, Cantara and her long-time guy friend grow closer. Nearing graduation, they both realize that they want to marry each other; yet, he is from a completely different "cast." She never planned to defy her parents, but knows that breaking the news of whom she wants to marry breaks centuries of tradition, culture, and family expectations; and, the news will be ill-received by her parents.

Cantara secures her first professional job in the U.S. and decides to fly to her homeland to spend a couple of months with her family before she starts working. She knows she has to deliver news that will send shockwaves throughout the family, and finds it difficult to gain the courage to have the discussion. Two weeks pass, then four, then six, when her "fiancé's" mother—who already knows the news—calls her mother to discuss the matter. Just as she expected, all hell breaks loose. Her family calls an "intervention" to figure out what they are going to do with her. Her father initially tries forceful intimidation, emotional blackmail, and guilt to convince her to change her mind. Cantara stands her ground; speaking up to her father for the first time ever.

Her parents confiscate her passport to prevent her from returning to the U.S., which she perceives as being held hostage, until she "comes to her senses" and follows tradition. Secretly, Cantara creates an escape plan, recruiting a friend to help. When her father realizes he cannot sway her, he comes to terms with her decision to return, and tells her through tears.

Upon returning to the U.S., the couple waits years to gain her parents' consent, which does not happen. The rift with her parents widens to a point where they are not on speaking terms. With all of this in mind, Cantara decides to wait no longer and marry her fiancé. His parents attend the wedding, but her parents refuse to attend, still in disapproval of the union. The wedding signifies a first for Cantara's family: she was the first to break cultural tradition and the social normalcy.

A month after the wedding, she receives a reconnecting call from her mother that instructs her, "Don't tell your dad." Interestingly, Cantara's sibling honored the normal tradition and it was not a good fit, whereas Cantara's marriage continues to flourish. Realizing that her decision shattered her parents' world, Cantara does not hold any anger with her parents.

Cantara realizes that she can accomplish anything after breaking major barriers, putting years of tradition on the line. She no longer feels she has to repress her "Alpha-ness." She is now the CEO of her own tech company based in the U.S.

What is the common bond these women throughout time share? They were trailblazers, bar setters, and leaders exhibiting multi-faceted powers and gifts, utilizing them via their minds, bodies, and souls among common men and nations. They were perceived as mutant females.

Mutants are noted for being a result of a change or alteration, deviating in form or nature. In this case, it is an organic infusion of selective male gender characteristics coupled with the sharpest female prowess, all embodied in the form of a woman—also known as an Alpha Female. This unique blend of traits, found in a very small percentage of the female population, makes these women a powerful force; thus, creating in others the overwhelming urges to silence them.

Alpha Females are the deviation from societal, normal females. Dating back centuries, to the inception of human civilization, female mutants have always existed and lived amongst normal society. Through the centuries, female mutants worked hard to blend in with humankind and not draw attention to their distinctive differences. They reluctantly—yet purposefully—silenced themselves in order to assimilate with societies' norms in an attempt to minimize the dreadful labeling by peers, community, or family members. They masked their mutation as a survival tactic to avoid being publically ridiculed, ostracized or, in the worst case, burned at the stake. During this time, no advocate supported them or spoke on their behalf about why and how they were so different. Instead, spiritual leaders prayed to remove their sins and cast away demons that resided within them. Despite numerous attempts, even alchemy and witchcraft proved to be unsuccessful at finding a cure for the abnormal—and, at the time, unacceptable—behavior. Unfortunately, many of them suffered in misery and even lost their lives. Primarily driven by the fear of the unparalleled power of smooth mental and sexual manipulation, fearlessness, resilience, visionary foresight, and heightened instinct, was society trying to force their kind into extinction?

Over many centuries, their mutation slowly became tolerated, but not always accepted. Even those brave enough to reveal their differences continued to carry the burden and could not continue to live quiet, normal lives. Although reigning authorities—like the church or government—no longer burned these women at the stake, society continued to ridicule them for being different. Protected by certain characteristics of their mutant gene, they persevered and ultimately helped pave the way for an easier existence for the future of their kind. In today's culture, these rare females continue to mask the unique gene, although it has become slightly more accepted. Now, these females are publically recognized; but, they continue to be habitually mislabeled and widely misunderstood.

Historically, male-dominated cultures required that women be seen and not heard; helpful, but not boisterous. Societal norms preferred and encouraged women to be soft, nurturing, loving, child-bearing creatures, placed on earth only to cater to significant others and family. Women had little say; and, on rare occasions when they did speak up, their opinions were rarely heard or taken seriously. They were maligned as acting out of character and, definitely, out of their boundaries. Woman's suffrage became the plight of the 1848 presidential campaign and it took a constitutional amendment in 1920 to grant women the right to vote. Women were little more than second-class citizens, required to submit to their male counterparts.

In this chapter, you will discover more about the mystery of the Alpha Female and begin to understand who she really is rather than what society mislabels her to be.

Mislabeled And Misunderstood

Within each species, certain animals, or humans, resonate as dominate. They are the "leaders of the pack." Typically, the one who displays the greatest dominance is a male. This leader, naturally or forcefully, takes the responsibility to direct, provide for, and protect those around him. The one who takes on this unassigned responsibility is typically referred to as the Alpha Male. Whether he fails or succeeds, the other members of the group recognize and reward him. They label him as brave. They identify and treat him like their leader. They grant him preferential access and rarely ridicule his approach, despite the number of casualties he may leave behind to accomplish his goal. Unfortunately, the

Alpha Male's counterpart, the Alpha Female, rarely gets depicted in the same positive light.

Remember, very few Alpha Females exist and their distinct gene mimics that of their male counterparts. However, where her counterpart is praised for his dominance, the Alpha Female has alternatively been mislabeled. Present-day labeling classifications include: bitch, bossy, lesbian, shrew, ball-buster, she-man, maverick, evil, high-maintenance, snob, aggressive, cold, and callous. There are more.

These labels place her in proverbial categorical boxes — partly because society does not understand her genetic wiring, nor know how to relate to her. Silently, they may fear her power.

The misconception of the underlying DNA of the mutant gene creates the illusion that she must be debauched or flawed because of these differences.

It doesn't help that the Alpha Female is depicted in popular media as "the successful career woman who is hard-nosed, snobby, cannot keep a man, and will die alone." This societal portrayal has unfortunately caused people to actually believe that there is something wrong with her because she does not align to the institutional model of what a woman *should* be. A few examples include a scene from the movie *The Best Man*. Here's the scene: The guys are playing cards one evening and they are having a discussion about their friend Jordan. One of them makes a remark that Jordan is extremely successful and makes a great living; she's strong, and is currently single. One would think that he is giving her kudos until this remark is made: "If she has all of that going and doing it by herself, then she is damn near lesbian." They all laugh in agreement and move on to another subject—as if a female couldn't possibly have it all.

In the movie, *Think Like a Man, Act Like a Lady*, based on the book by Steve Harvey, the one character that is portrayed to be the Alpha Female, Lauren, is made to feel as if there is something wrong with her because she has high standards and expectations for the man she desires as a companion. She is the one woman—given her executive CEO position and successful career—that actually thinks and moves like a man, but is slammed for it in the movie. It is illustrated that she is *superficially* attracted to the Alpha Male, a college friend, who is a corporate executive and her equal in every manner. Unfortunately, the movie does a poor depiction of illustrating her true attraction which is to his intellect, success and powerful prowess. When she breaks up with Dominic—the story's dreamer who desires to become a chef—to pursue the Alpha Male, she feeds him lines that a man would say to a woman. "Dominic, I'm gonna hit you with the headline, okay?" She explains that she has recently reconnected with an ex-boyfriend from college, and so on. When Dominic asks, "You breaking up with me," she replies, "No, I'm not breaking up, just taking a break. I need some space." It is at this moment that Dominic accuses her of "sounding like a guy." Then she hits him with the typical male, *"I really like you, did not want to string you along, and can we be friends" script.* She compartmentalized the situation and handled him like a business decision. This style and way of thinking is usually attributed to a man's style; yet, it really isn't acceptable for a woman to "think like a man" despite Harvey's position, given the movie title. Later in the movie, it's revealed that Lauren would be happier with Dominic, the Beta Male; teaching her the lesson to not be stuck on the high standard that she had set before. This "settling" advice is even given to her by her Beta Female friend, Candace. This is shown in a scene when Candace and Lauren are having a conversation about Steve Harvey's book. Lauren asks Candace "Why should I have to lower my standards to get a man? I want my equal. Or at least an attractive, cultured man who is over six feet tall, makes six figures, and isn't intimidated by my success." Candace quotes from the book, *"Strong, independent, and lonely women..."* where she points out that strong and independent women end up lonely. She then tells Lauren that she is a bitch and too strong. Why is Lauren's friend trying to get her to lower her standards and looking upon her as being too strong, a bitch, or like a man? To top it all off, Lauren, the portrayed egotistical and superficial CEO has to be knocked off of her high horse and "taught a lesson." Why couldn't the movie show Lauren being happy with the Alpha Male? Does she need to lower, or change, her standards to not be lonely, and to be fulfilled according to society's standards? Is this the message that really needs to be sent to women?

Let's now address the myth that "strong and independent women are lonely women." They do not equate at all. Just because women are <u>alone</u> does not mean that they are <u>lonely</u>. These are two completely different states of being.

In the movie *Disclosure*, there are two Alpha Females, both highly successful in their careers: Meredith and Stephanie. Meredith, who is under deposition for sexual harassment, makes the best statement on society and Alpha Female: *"I am a sexually aggressive woman. I like it.... It is the same damn thing sense the beginning of time. Veil it, hide it, lock it up, and throw away the key. We expect a woman to do a man's job, make a man's money, and then walk around with a parasol, and lie down for a man to fuck her like it was still 100 years ago? Well, no thank you!"*

However, the one that truly ends up winning is Stephanie, who is portrayed as having more nurturing characteristics, given she has a son and played more of a background role until the end. This still depicts the stereotype that a nice, acceptable Alpha Female is the one that has a child and/or a husband, conforming to social normality; while the other is the hard core Alpha Female who is feminine, sexually powerful, has no children, no spouse, has a top position, and is deemed as evil. How interesting is this message? This portrayal has not only taken place in movies, but in television shows as well, such as *How to Get Away with Murder*. Annalise Keating is portrayed as the "woman who cannot be touched and a chess master of movements and people; she's on the top of her game in her professional life, yet has the worst personal life. She is portrayed as the sociopathic, opportunistic, man–stealing bitch and yet she cannot have it all to be happy. It's almost as if society is trying to embrace the Alpha Female by recognizing her existence, but still depicting her as if she cannot have it all and socially demoralizing Alpha Females to still keep them in their place.

One television sitcom that was revolutionary and a better depiction of the Alpha Female was *Murphy Brown*. She had her inner demons, but was portrayed in a much more respectful manner, even in how she handled her flaws. She was the highest ranking journalist who broke the glass ceiling for women in the profession, commanded everyone's attention, was always the go-to person for advice and leadership, would outwit the guys, would not back down from any challenge, could be the tomboy, yet was always exquisitely dressed and never lost her femininity. Many revered her, the Alpha Males loved her, and the Beta men and women feared her. However, this Alpha Female character made revolutionary real headlines in the 1992 Presidential campaign when Vice President Dan Quayle criticized the character for "mocking the importance of fathers by bearing her child alone" during his speech at the

Common Wealth Club in San Francisco, sparking a public discussion on family values.

With labels and depictions such as these, it is no wonder that since the early days of humanity to present day, Alpha Females work so hard to mask their mutation to appear normal so that they are not ostracized. It lends one to ask: If the Alpha Female is the female mirror of the Alpha Male, why aren't the Alpha Males labeled, described, and treated in the same manner? Yes, we live in a double standard society, but is it truly a stretch of the imagination to accept that a female can be alpha?

To clarify, being "diagnosed" as having an A-Type personality or holding a high level-leadership position in an organization does not equate to being Alpha.

According to *Dictionary.com*, the definition of "Alpha" is "being the most dominant, powerful, or assertive person in a particular group. *See also Alpha Male.*" The Alpha Female is only mentioned in a definition in reference to the animal kingdom—elephants as an example. Webster references Alpha Male and defines it as "having the most power in a group of animals or people;" there is no mention of Alpha Female. *Dictionary.com* mentions Alpha Female as being the dominant in the pack only in reference to the animal kingdom, and only references her in the human kingdom by linking it to the Alpha Girl, which has a negative definition of being a "mean girl or a bully."

Alternatively, *Dictonary.com* defines the Alpha Male as being the most powerful, dominate, or assertive man in a group. These reputable sources help perpetuate the perception that the Alpha Female only exists in the animal kingdom and only exists as a "girl" that is deliberately mean and a bully in the human species. Interestingly enough, we are teaching little girls the same thing by calling them "bossy" and creating a society where we are subconsciously suppressing future female leaders, scientists, politicians from adolescence.

Let's set the record straight by relabeling her appropriately. The Alpha Female *is* dominant, powerful, and assertive, just as her Alpha Male counterpart. However, society has shown and led people to believe that "real" women are not supposed to be any of those things as those qualities are not considered feminine.

One of the main traits of the Alpha Female is her unspoken power: She dominates, but is not domineering; she asserts, but is not necessarily aggressive; she may not be the prettiest in the room, but she is the most beautiful. "Pretty" is superficial; but, "beauty" radiates from within and radiates through how she speaks, stands, stares, smiles, walks, and gestures. She takes the rules into consideration, but blazes her own path. Her mind calculates and compartmentalizes thoughts similar to her male counterpart, which gives her the ability to easily and quickly emotionally detach from a situation to make a decision and or take the lead. She does not adhere to the social norms of religion, marriage, and children. She commands the attention of others with her presence, and has great situational awareness to quickly adapt to her surroundings. She's a chameleon. She never has to state who she is or the fact that she is an Alpha Female; it's obvious and unspoken. So what makes her this way? Is it her DNA? What is the X factor? Is it her unspoken power?

Reflect on the biblical story of the original Alpha Female, Eve. It is told, acknowledged, and accepted that Eve, the first woman, was created from the rib of the first man, Adam, meaning she was second to man. From that point, women were deemed the "weaker" sex. However, Eve's unspoken power influenced Adam to take a bite of the forbidden fruit. So who had the real power in that relationship? Who was truly the Alpha? The "unspoken power" can be used for *good* or *ill* intent, but the fact remains that it does exist.

Look back at other Alpha Females throughout history: Queen Nefertiti, Amelia Earhart, Condoleezza Rice, Maya Angelou and Oprah Winfrey. What do all of these women have in common? Yes, they have all made large impacts on the world and history. Yes, they all have fame to their name. Yes, they were all successful in their moment in time. However, that is not the "tie" that binds them. Part of the tie that binds them is a regal aura that naturally exudes from them. Many women try to emulate, but cannot quite duplicate this aura; often giving true Alpha Females a bad rap. **True Alpha Females are the essence of inner *beauty*,** unspoken *power* and have the fire of purpose in their *soul* that can never be extinguished.

Given the elements that radiate from these women among the dark and derogatory labeling that has been perpetuated, let the record be corrected and let's "re-label" them properly to be referred to as *exactly* what they are: ALPHA FEMALES.

If, by this time, you are not fully aware of the significant imbalance of the direct and subliminal messages of societal acceptance and views between the Alpha Female and her male counterpart, take a reflective moment to really think about what *you* have personally seen, heard, perceived, or thought about Alpha Females before you read the rest of this book. Ask yourself: "Were those that I described as such *really* Alpha Females, or were they something else?"

The following chapters provide insight into the various aspects of the Alpha Female's life, experiences, emotions (yes, she has emotions, she's not emotional), strengths and weaknesses, while exploring the mutant X-factor gene. This book lends this gene the name of "AMtrogen-8."

CHAPTER TWO

From α to Alpha: She's Born, Not Made

Despite the limited exploration and thorough examination of the Alpha Female, there is an understanding that she is not the typical societal female. Alpha Females may spring from parents who are both Alpha, one is Alpha, or neither of them are Alpha. She may derive from various backgrounds, cultures, or social economic areas. Given the various possible combinations of environment, upbringing, and parental traits, common questions that are posed on this topic arise: Is the Alpha Female born or made? If she is born this way, why? If she is made (given her environment, situation, upbringing), then how?

The "Absolute 8," The "Augmented 8" and The "Non-8"

A frequent question posed on the topic of Alpha Females asks: "Is she born or made?" This question rarely, if ever, seeps from the lips of society any longer when it comes to the Alpha Male or alphas in the animal kingdom. Society accepts they arrive into the world to dominate and lead the pack. It is simply accepted as the norm.

Evaluation of various women on their experiences, beliefs, behaviors, backgrounds, cultures, ages, successes, setbacks, relationships, parental rearing, economic status, physical attributes, and environment brought very clear distinctions in addressing the "born vs. made" inquiry. The

"True 8" classification theory creates a mental visual to communicate an understanding of the distinctions between the "born" Alpha Female, the "non-born but perceived" Alpha Female, and the non-Alpha Female. Alpha or non-Alpha, born or perceived, does not equate to better or worse, good or bad. The differences are highlighted, acknowledged, and respected, given people are created differently.

The number "8" has been chosen to represent the Alpha Female because, based on numerology and numerical analysis, it spiritually signifies: natural-born leadership, success, authority, power, self-confidence, dominance, drive, presence, and non- emotional, and is the highest feminine number.

The number "8" is comprised of two perfect loops, or circles, and when turned horizontally forms the infinity symbol. The Alpha Female consistently strives for excellence, while her core beliefs, calculating mindset, and commanding presence are impermeably infinite.

Alpha Females who are "born that way" are classified as "Absolute 8." Whether raised in a two-parent home, a single-parent home, an affluent household, or economically challenged household, their behaviors, beliefs, desires, and thought process are engrained at day one and never waiver. External experiences and influential relationships shape portions of their situational filtering, but their core drive, internal wiring and beliefs remain unaffected. Whether they are raised with dominating parents, or with a strict religious structure, or in an abusive environment – or the opposite of these – the external forces exhibit a placebo effect on the

"Absolute 8." These females exhibit common behaviors, such as:

- Extreme focus; single-mindedness
- Athleticism
- Career focused - being part of their identity
- Not wanting to be tied down
- Higher sexual libido; ability to enjoy one-night-stands with no regrets
- Emotionally self-sufficient
- Fiercely independent
- Naturally command attention when entering a room
- Stealthy movements
- Self-aware; use deliberate body language to give non-verbal cues
- Doesn't give a shit about other people's approval
- Normally exudes a presence of purpose
- Her ring finger may be longer than her index finger, indicating higher levels of testosterone
- Ability to resist pressure from social conventions like marriage, religion, government, or having children
- Identifies/acknowledges other Alpha Females in social and/or business settings; non-threatened

On the fascia, the "Augmented 8" carries many of the characteristics of the "Absolute 8" Alpha Female. The "Augmented 8" shines successfully, carries herself well in social and business settings, exerts independence, focuses on her career, and, from the outside world, looks like an "Absolute 8." The "Augmented 8" derives from the external forces that augment her behaviors, thoughts, actions, responses, and results that align with the characteristics of the 'Absolute 8" Alpha Female. The "Augmented 8" is born into this world as something different, perhaps a "6" or a "7" by nature. Given her situation, upbringing, external influences, or maybe a traumatic experience, the "6" or "7" adds what she needs to survive and flourish. As an example, if born a "6," then the adjustment of "2" is added to augment the behavior and create the 8-like effect. Likewise, if born a "7" then there is a slight adjustment of "1." Therefore, many of the "Absolute 8" Alpha Female characteristics and behaviors are realized. If they both look like an "8", then what is the difference?

The "Absolute 8" is hard-wired with beliefs, values, physical, and genetic differences from birth. The "Augmented 8" is coded differently and soft-wired such that, if not for a certain type of external force, many "Augmented 8s" openly admit that they would have taken a completely different direction. If external forces cause a "6" or "7" to become a "4" or "5," they adjust to be more of a Beta Female. "Absolute 8" Alpha Females express a consistent story of "I was born like this" or "I've been this way since birth."

"Absolute 8" Alpha Females admit needing to repress their alpha traits for a short time based upon their environment; but, the alpha remains only to emerge more forcefully later. For example, the "Absolute 8" may be raised in a very strict household where she is forced to wear certain clothing and to be "seen and not heard." Yet, outside the household, she has the freedom to showcase her true personality – and does. "Augmented 8s" openly express the

26

consistent message of "I became this way because of… [situation X]," or "[Situation Y] made me this way, when I was…"

The "Non-8" females, also known as Beta Females, exhibit contrasting characteristics of the Alpha Female. The behaviors, mannerisms, beliefs, thinking styles, need for validation and relationship management oppose those of the Alpha Female. The contrast simply signifies the difference between them and does not indicate less value. The "Non-8" female is not as stealthy as the Alpha Female and, oftentimes, their movements can be predicted. "Non-8" females who try to emulate the "Absolute 8" or "Augmented 8" may be viewed as the female who is trying too hard to fit in, to be liked, or to be heard.

What happens when newly "Authenic-8" enters the world?

Congrats, It's a Girl! But…

Baby Channing leaves the hospital with her proud, first-time, parents; swaddled in a pink blanket, with a cute pink and white headband on her hairless head, ensuring the world knows their baby girl arrived.

Channing's parents dote over her day and night, watching her sit up, crawl and take her first steps within the first nine months of her life. Her parents are proud and have filled her room with stuffed animals and her initial set of toys. On Channing's first birthday, her mother presents her with a cute doll for her to hug, love, and nurture — or so she thinks. Her mother gasps when Channing takes one look at the doll and shows no interest at all. Her mother pleads with her to take the doll and assumes that, once she has it in her arms, the female "nurturing" instinct will take over. Wrong! Channing embraces the doll for a few seconds to stop her mother's pleading, and then tosses it across the room, never looking back. Channing's mom encounters this scenario more times in the next year only to have the same result. Channing hates baby dolls. Channing chooses to play with blocks and the car toys that belong to her male cousins. Her father does not make a big deal out of it, but her mother cannot understand why her baby girl has no interest in "girly" toys and wonders if this is normal or if there is something wrong with Channing. Her parents realize that their "baby girl" is not the "typical girl" that they thought they brought home from the hospital.

By the time Channing is age four, she makes it clear to her parents that she is more interested in playing with "boy" toys and electronic games, she likes rough housing, and she prefers not to wear dresses. If she wears a skirt, she must wear shorts underneath so that she can play on the monkey bars at the playground. Channing leads the kids in her nursery school class and some call her bossy. She excels in all of the activities and can even keep up with the boys in sports. Her dad embraces it as he gets a baby girl that likes what he likes; almost like a son.

Channing continues becoming more of a tomboy. She climbs trees, plays kickball and basketball, has some girlfriends but refuses to play with dolls or sit for a tea party. She plays with video games, remote control cars, and chemistry sets; her parents notice that she has a knack for taking everything apart to find out how it operates, and for putting it back together. During the summer while school is out, she follows her father to work to learn what he does for a living, *sitting in on meetings and learning the business. She also tags along with her father to his acquaintances' residences, where her calculating instinct hints that the situation is weird, but dismisses it to play with the surrounding children or to self-entertain.*

Every new mother and father of a baby girl takes her home from the hospital wrapped in a pink blanket, showing the world that she is filled with "sugar and spice and everything nice," because this is what society dictates that females are from birth. However, some parents soon discover their baby girl thinks, behaves, speaks, carries themselves and even plays differently than other girls. As they watch her grow, her parents recognize that her way of thinking reflects *her* beliefs, and she possesses a *trait* they are incapable of constraining or changing.

Undeniable common characteristics among those girls exist pertaining to how they socially interact with their peers, the peers they gravitate toward, what they play with, who they play with, how they handle emotions, and the role they play in social groups. Many of the commonalities among these girls in the early formative years are:

- Walking and talking earlier than their peer group
- Showing early assertion of independence and autonomy
- Being disinterested in dolls or other "girl" toys. If they play with dolls, they create scenarios where the female doll does not hold traditional female roles; if she has an Easy Bake Oven®, she uses it for experiments—not to bake a cake

- Preferring to play with "boy" toys, like race cars, building blocks, and electronic games
- Preferring to play with the boys rather than with the girls, as boys are more likely engaged in sports or rough housing
- Exhibiting high logical thinking and reasoning that is most attributed to their male peers; the "lawyer" of the household
- Challenging authority and the status quo
- Possessing a high level of competitiveness, willing to attempt to do what girls are not *supposed* to be able to do
- Leading her pack of peers
- Taking risks in school and play
- Despising dresses and frilly clothing
- Getting her peers to work for her

These common qualities, characteristics and interactions start early in life. At this point, parents may question why their little girl does not show interest in the stereotypical girl things. These traits strengthen, evolve, and grow as the young girl matures. Parents, do not be alarmed. Instead, recognize her for who she is and nurture her to harness the power she possesses. Do not attempt to force her into a social-gender-behavior box.

"Tomboy" to Awakening

Channing continuing to mature, hangs with the guys, befriends a few girls, enhances her athletic scorecard, and continues to excel in school. *As she enters puberty, her body and looks blossom into womanhood. She notices the change, her parents notice the change, and boys notice the change.*

By the time Channing attends high school, she leads various school clubs, plays sports, excels academically, and exudes the confidence and beauty that has boys constantly at her front door. Channing laid out her plans for college, her career, and what life looks like 20 years down the road: successful, likely unmarried, no children. Her parents continually boast and brag on her accomplishments and well-rounded performance. Channing hones in on her femininity and sexuality. She realizes that she can hang with the boys and think like them, be feminine like the girls, and easily compartmentalizes both. She accepts dates from various guys, as she loves to have fun. All the while a particular memory daunts her: the "acquaintances" her father would introduce to her. She then realizes they were his mistresses and wonders if her mother knew about the infidelity. Channing, being the logical lawyer from birth, feels compelled to broach the subject with her mother but knows that, depending on the answer, she would either question her mother's blindness to the situation, or judge her for accepting the treatment of being less than number one and the only one. This realization crushes most girls, but Channing quickly compartmentalizes the situation, the relationship with her father, and adjusts in an Alpha-like manner. Channing makes an internal pact that she would never be treated as second best.

Channing places guys on her social calendar as a transactional slot in time. She pays more attention to one of the guys on her dating roster and develops feelings for him. She keeps her goals in mind, but realizes she cares for him more than the others and is sexually attracted to him. Channing maintains control in every aspect of her life, even at this stage. She has known the guy since they were in nursery school. She makes the decision that he is "the one," the one to be her first. This friend, Jackson, is a little older than Channing and has always had a secret crush on her. One night out, she allows Jackson to believe he initiated the intimate sexual event, all the while, Channing seduced Jackson, including taking a "controlling position." She never reveals to him that he was her first lover as she believes that the information would create a shift in power. Soon thereafter, Jackson professes his love to her and informs her she is "the one" for him, but Channing has already compartmentalized the fact that, while she cares for him deeply, she is not in love with him. Channing quickly gives Jackson the "It's not you, it's me...we can still be friends" speech. Jackson, having used that speech on girls himself, accuses Channing of "acting like a guy."

As the young Alpha Female (α), matures into puberty, her traits continue to mature as well. She does not necessarily shed her ability to hang with the guys; however, there is more self-awareness of her femininity. Remember, Alpha Females maintain their femininity although they possess and display Alpha Male-type traits. By this time in her lifecycle, she notices that she is different from her female peers, but she's not sure why. She evolves from being "one of the guys" to "the one guys notice." She vaguely learns and leverages her power of seduction (sexual and non-sexual), of both guys and girls to influence those around her. This starts a confusing time for the Alpha Female as she begins to receive both high kudos and high criticism from her peers. Given her intellect, sharp wit, drive to excel, ability to compartmentalize her emotions, athletic ability, her ability to compete with the guys (and in some areas outperform them), and the overall presence that she brings when commanding attention in a room, creates the "love to hate her" relationships. Many of the commonalities exhibited among the Alpha Female in this stage are:

- Holding leadership positions with her sports teams, social groups and school clubs
- Keeping a full schedule: part-time job, full social calendar, community service
- Needing to excel in academics and all other challenges
- Disguising and hiding vulnerability
- Becoming a "chameleon" among her peers; hanging with the guys, yet adjusting her style when with her female friends
- Preferring to have more male friends
- Thinking outside the box about relationships, marriage, children; not conforming to social norms
- Exploiting the weaknesses of others and uses them to her competitive advantage
- Being extremely focused on what she wants in life

In addition to these common traits is another type of awareness that takes place within the Alpha Female: her sexuality, sexual power, and prowess. In evaluating Alpha Females and their beta female counterparts, there is a definite distinction of the "control factor" in this arena. Given Alpha Females "think like a man," they can quickly compartmentalize their feelings in this area. She resists peer pressure, but will definitely identify when it is the right time for her "first time." She controls the situation by allowing the guy to believe he is in control, but all the while she has compartmentalized the situation on what she wants to do and why. She may feel that she is "in love" with the guy or may want the physical relationship without the emotional tie. She also discovers that her libido level is the same of her male counterpart, if not higher. Because society teaches "girls" that they should not be sexual beings or they will be labeled as a whore, many Alpha Females temporarily repress their desires at this stage in their life. The ones that don't are wrongfully characterized as being *fast* or *loose*. Interestingly, their male counterparts at this stage are encouraged to embrace their sexual desires and "become men." Beta females may be more inclined to make sexual decisions due to peer pressure or to please the guy she likes. The Alpha Females that do not repress their libido are more "stealthy" in their execution. She shows very little vulnerability to the emotional connection she may have with the guy she chooses to be intimate with. She disarms the partner she chooses to be intimate with from having this level of control, even at this early stage in her life. Beta female peers tend to directly contrast this behavior.

The Collegiate Chameleon

Channing attends a prestigious university and majors in a male-dominated field. She holds a leadership position in her nationally known sorority. She belongs to various school, social, and professional organizations, aware of the networks they build and to give back to the community. She creates close-knit bonds with a few of her sorority sisters, which are the most girlfriends she's had in her life. Once again, many of her peers gravitate toward her and she takes on the "protector" role over those for whom she cares. Channing's direct approach and blunt conversation style strain some of the friendships she holds dear.

When it comes to the guys on and off campus, many want to have the opportunity to date Channing, but only a select few make the cut. She continues to have guy friends that are strictly platonic. This also strains some of her friendships because, even in this stage, she would rather hang with the guys. From the dating perspective, Channing prides herself on being a "serial monogamous" dater when, in reality, she keeps a full social calendar and a roster of datable guys. At times, she dates multiple men and the majority of them cater to her schedule and wants.

To ensure that she is on track with her goals, Channing reviews her life and career plan, which she started before college, to evaluate the next steps. Channing continually focuses on the big picture. She knows where she is going and what she wants out of life, and embraces ideas on how to get there. Her views on marriage, kids, and female roles in society and the corporate world are solidified.

She plans to capture the executive corner office by the time she is thirty and will stop nothing short of reaching that goal-at any cost.

During her senior year in college, Channing runs into a familiar face, Jackson. He acknowledges her slightly, remembering their last rendezvous. Jackson unaffectionate and callous interaction intrigues Channing. Whether her ego takes over or her Alpha traits heighten, Channing challenges herself to regain the relationship with Jackson. After a little time of them hanging out, Channing "gets what she wants" by having Jackson back in her life.

As graduation approaches, her hard work and focus pays off. Channing draws attention from many major companies soliciting her to join their firm. The most lucrative offer includes her moving to a different state and a large amount of international and domestic travel. Jackson works locally and his career is slowly moving forward as well. Channing has a dilemma as she and Jackson are now a couple and she finally admits to herself that she has deeper feelings for him. In addition to the dilemma, Channing discovers that she is pregnant. She thinks to herself for a second: "Does she follow the societal influence (or her heart) to live life with a husband and child, or her logical mind to continue to focus and meet her goals?" Although not the easiest of decisions, Channing chooses to dissolve the relationship and abort the pregnancy without hesitation or remorse. She knows deep down that marriage and children are not in her plan and not what she wants at this time, if ever. Channing's parents raised her in a Christian home, but the religious beliefs do not deter her decision. Channing compartmentalizes the dissolved relationship and the terminated pregnancy, regroups, and accepts the lucrative offer which puts her on her path to success.

The adult Alpha Female within strongly emerges during the end of the collegiate stage. She learns to fine-tune the differences that separate her from other females, thus creating the chameleon persona that carries her forth throughout her existence. The "Collegiate Chameleon" persona allows the Alpha Female to appear *normal* to her peers, while navigating the collegiate jungle. She focuses on the finish line with laser precision. She:

- Completes a competitive, heavily male-dominated curriculum with high academic performance
- Achieves high social status on campus
- Leads organizations
- Devises a social network of males and females
- Executes her career plan

Once the laser beam focus activates, very little to nothing stands in her way, which some perceive as being "cold" and "unemotional." The beliefs she formed at the adolescent stage solidifies as her platform by which she guides herself, assesses her peers, and chooses her lovers. Her beliefs contradict many of the widely accepted female norms that society imposes upon women. Her chameleon-like instinct drives her to stealthily tone down certain actions and behaviors based upon her beliefs. The double-edged sword that scores the Alpha Female is that no matter the effort expended to disguise her "mutation," it eventually permeates in its raw and natural form. She balances her interactions to appear normal while holding true to her non-traditional beliefs, such as:

- Keeping two to three guys on her dating roster; she does not sleep with all of them
- Joining a heavily female-populated organization, like a sorority, to have female friends; she'd rather be with the guys
- Avoiding relationship commitments or children
- Being spiritual, but not ruled by religion
- Being protective of her close friends
- Leveraging her intellect, beauty, and sexuality to command a scene, control the room, and seduce men and women politically and professionally

Some of these actions alone gain her negative attention by those around her, although it would not for a male counterpart. She gives less than a damn about what others think about her. However, she camouflages her innate attitude to influence others' perceptions, strengthen her personal brand, and, ultimately, accomplish her goals. Upon college graduation, the Alpha Female poises herself to what she believes "it takes" to take the world by storm.

Her lack of knowledge to what lies ahead for her in corporate America—the pedestal and the dungeon given her rare existence—bring forth an unbridled reality.

CHAPTER THREE

The Boardroom Bitch

Alpha Females can be team players; however, their main focus is on the "i." It's the "i" in *strategic* and *politics* that vie for the ultimate *win*. Female corporate executives are expected to play in a male-dominated arena. To "win," she must deliver results, navigate the politics, and show no emotion; at all of which the Alpha Female excels. Alpha Females making it amongst the executive ranks have mastered those factors to gain respect of, and compete with, the big boys. Many believe in winning at all costs—but do they *really* understand the price they pay? What is the perception of her while climbing the corporate ladder or when she reaches various levels?

Most women who assert their power of authority in an organization are labeled as "bitchy," "bossy," or "Type A," or are accused of *sleeping their way to the top*. Their intellect and adaptability are acknowledged only secondarily as *"Yes, she has those too."* These labels come from both women and men; oftentimes more from women. In contrast, men in positions of power are labeled as a "respected prick," or *the guy who made it because he was confident, a real go-getter who took risks.* Despite how much of an asshole a man may have been to get into that powerful position, he is neither questioned nor challenged, but rather rewarded.

41

Although many women in high-ranking positions are automatically labeled as "Alpha," the two do not correlate. Most Alpha Females align themselves into positions of power, but many females that are in powerful positions are not Alphas; they are simply in powerful positions; the same can be said for their male counterparts. The differences are highlighted based on their reactions and handling of high pressure and critical situations, either corporate or personal. It is easy to tap their insecurities and fragile egos, they are the first to react in self-preservation to crisis situations, and are they easily threatened by perceived competition, especially another female or a true Alpha Female.

Some authors recommend that women *"lean in"* or *"act like a lady, think like a man."* However, do Alpha Females who already possess those strong traits get placed on a pedestal in the corporate world—or are they condemned?

Corporate Seductress or Corporate Seduced? Part 1

Channing, knowing her high potential status within the company, receives her first invitation to an elite corporate social event. Realizing the opportunities to showcase her power-networking capability and build her corporate social capital, she plans her attire, identifies individuals on whom she plans to focus her attention, and maps information she intends to mentally collect from the event.

During the two weeks leading to the event, Channing continues executing her role as a young employee, while keeping her focus on the path to success. She invites a few of her peers, Jace,

Corbin, and Landri, to dinner to get to know them better. Jace's mother holds an executive position in another business unit; Corbin was recently recognized for solving a major issue for the business; and Landri holds the president position of the junior employee resource group. Channing encourages them to order what they desire—she's covering the expense—impressing them. By the end of the first round of drinks, the group shares stories of their lives, professional careers, and goals. Channing mentions an innovative idea she formulated, draws the group's attention to how it meets their goals, utilizes their individual strengths, highlights her admiration for them, and feeds their egos in garnering their support. She uses her words, slight touching gestures with the men, and the sisterhood connection with Landri, thus creating the seductive vision. The invitees pledge their support to Channing's idea and leadership.

She meets with her "crew" over the next week and a half to work on the idea. The team shapes the idea into an initial tangible reality, creating excitement for the members and buzz of notoriety among their peers and leadership, bolstering Channing's seductive ego.

The night of the corporate social arrives. Channing enters the venue, stunning as usual, and quickly assesses the ambiance and the people in the arena. She makes her way to an area of the venue where many of the individuals she has targeted to network are gathered. Attendance by executive leadership—representing corporate and individual business units—compliments the *exquisitely decorated arena, fine cuisine, and expensive champagne, thus creating an air of elitism and power.*

Executively poised, Channing greets many of the top executives, spending no more than 10 to 15 minutes among each "networked" circle as to ensure she makes herself available, but not in surplus. Various leaders approach to congratulate her on the innovative project that she leads, requesting she present it to various executive leadership teams. She gladly accepts. During the kudos given to her, Corbin repeatedly motions to Channing, inviting her to visit with her peers. Channing gestures, signaling "in a minute," as each leader introduces her to another leadership circle. One of those leadership circles contains Jace's mother, Catherine, who resides on the West Coast. Catherine warmly smiles, comments on the stellar performance of Channing and the team. She invites Channing to get on her calendar for a meeting to discuss her career aspirations and possible upcoming opportunities. Channing shares the great experiences obtained working with Jace. After a few minutes of small talk, the two ladies maneuver themselves to other areas of the venue.

Channing, deciding she has accomplished her mission for the night by investing more than two hours at the event, leaves. Corbin realizes she exited without acknowledging him or their peers. Others observed the "oversight," creating another buzz later in the evening.

What buzz stirred up later that evening? Was Channing the seducer or the one seduced?

Alpha Females are highly driven and focused. This attribute creates a double-edged sword when poorly managed and executed. The delicate balancing of the Alpha Female's ego, her influential abilities, her strategic thinking, emotional detachment, and focused execution, requires unbridled power at all times. An imbalance of any, especially ego, causes her to be blindsided by her own strengths. [Note: Younger Alpha Females, starting their careers, are more at risk. They adjust using past experiences believing they're a chess master, not realizing when they allow themselves to be the pawn.]

Influencing her peers comes as second nature to her. She chooses the right combination of peer collaboration to ensure success. Although she does protect those who are loyal to her, her actions are calculated based on perception, excellence, and/or purpose. Her peers may perceive her as a "user" rather than influencer if she allows her ambition to overshadow the big picture purpose. In many cases she is all about "her," but expects that others have to be about her as well, which creates distrust among her peers. The "user" or "all about me" perception may perpetuate beyond her peers to the various leadership, putting her fragile social network at high risk. Her ambition, coupled with her unawareness of an overexposed ego, becomes her Achilles heel, therefore making her the puppet instead of the puppet master. She becomes a major target of the corporate "smile- fuck."

Caution: The Alpha Female only has to realize that she has been bitten once for her to adjust, recompose, and execute the path to undo/mitigate the damage. When she realizes she has been "smile fucked," she masters the method for future use.

The Queen B: Can There "B" More Than One?

Channing continues her navigation through the waters of corporate America. Her performance has led to many successes and management has taken notice. Channing is creating her space in the "good ol' boy" circle, or so she thinks. She has worked her way from an intern to a full-time employee in an elite leadership development program to a middle management position. Although she experienced obstacles along her journey, she continues to observe the "unspoken rules of the company," learning from her experiences and adjusting accordingly. Channing creates many advocates at the company, but also picked up a few adversaries along the way. She is on the fast track in her career, beating all odds. Many people in her network compare her to woman named Kendall, who has been with the company seven years longer than Channing and also is viewed as a young up-and-comer.

Years later, Channing bumps into Kendall at a corporate event. Kendall, much like Channing, always performs well for the organization and had gained notoriety. The two ladies now work for the same division and share some of the same network of acquaintances.

Kendall still holds a higher position than Channing. She acknowledges the positive "buzz" on Channing and looks forward to seeing her in action again. Neither of them realizes that their paths are going to cross in a manner that will test their true Alphaism.

One particular day, Channing receives a phone call to report to the divisional vice-president's office. Channing meets with the vice president and he relays good news: Channing is being promoting to be on his leadership team as one of his directors. Channing gladly accepts the offer, given the position creates another accomplishment on her path to success. She knows the company wants more females in executive leadership positions. The promotion makes Channing the youngest member of the leadership team in both career years and age. She and Kendall are now peers on the same leadership team, reporting to the same vice-president. They are the only two women on the team.

The vice-president announces Channing's movement to the new position. The team welcomes Channing with open arms — most of them. Kendall, although somewhat pleased another female joined the team, formulates perceptions about the intent of the addition.

Channing hits the ground running with her new duties. She manages a functional department and the vice-president pairs her with Kendall to work on a special project that has extreme visibility to the corporate-level executives. She and Kendall, both rising stars, flawlessly execute the project exceeding the company's expectations, with the meticulous view of the "big picture" ensuring every detail aligns.

The male leadership team members notice the great job that they are doing. One male in particular, John, who has his eye on his next position, takes Kendall to lunch to "congratulate" her on her success with the project. John makes a point to highlight the stellar job that Channing did as well. He comments on Channing's intelligence, youth, executive presence, and desire to be successful. John slyly hints to Kendall that Channing is a likely contender for the next leadership position in the company. Kendall agrees with his first set of comments, but inquires on the latter. She reminds him of her seniority and successes thus far.

The next week, John approaches Channing at one of the company's social events, whispering much of the same "kudos" and thoughts about Kendall that he has shared with Kendall about Channing. Channing shows generous support of Kendall with John, boasting Kendall's performance and intellect. Channing agrees with John and acknowledges that both she and Kendall are great leaders and would be successful in their next role.

As time continues, Channing begins to notice a difference in Kendall. They are planning to present the project results to the corporate executives. Channing makes recommendations to Kendall on the presentation approach, based upon past experiences and research. Kendall quickly reminds her of her fairly new appointment to the leadership team in an attempt to dismiss Channing's recommendations. Kendall continues to attempt to undermine Channing's performance and contribution to the project and team. Channing notices Kendall's "under the bus" behavior; she then

48

takes steps to ensure no damage occurs to her, her reputation, or the project.

During the project presentation, Kendall continuously attempts to talk over Channing during her portion of the presentation, ensuring the leadership understands her role in the results. Channing stays on course, keeps her composure, and closes the presentation showcasing the leadership of the team effort and success. The corporate executives are on board and comment on the stellar results of the project. The feedback around areas of improvements actually aligned with the original recommendations Channing previously submitted to Kendall. Channing takes the high road by thanking the corporate executives for their feedback and is elated with their approval of the project results.

Back at the office, Channing realizes Kendall may not be the ally she expected. She continues to be respectful and cordial, but keeps a closer eye on the environment surrounding her and Kendall. Kendall notices the slight adjustment in Channing's behavior and invites her to lunch. During lunch, Kendall decides to lay down the law, informing Channing that she believes her advancement was premature, questioning her intellect and stating her opinion that the board would never consider her to be the next executive at such a young age. Kendall defends the poor decisions she made on the presentation, although she admittedly knows the feedback clearly aligned with Channing's advice. Kendall quickly advises Channing there will be "only one woman promoted" and it would more than likely be her.

Channing sits back in her seat for a short pause, then leans forward. As Channing leans in, she calmly and assuredly informs Kendall that there can be more than one woman at the top. She continues to inform Kendall that she may be a young professional, but she's a professional nonetheless, and is to be respected as such. Channing, realizing that Kendall perceives her as a threat, shares this with Kendall, along with the fact she knows of the "seeds" that were planted by John to create the tension and friction between them. She informs Kendall she is disappointed that Kendall fell for those planted seeds and was not strong enough to see past them. Channing discloses to Kendall someone attempted to plant those same seeds with her, but she did allow it to affect her relationship or support of Kendall. She concludes the conversation by sharing that other strong women are not intimidating to her; she embraces and supports them. Kendall's expression immediately becomes one of "Damn, I was played like a fuckin' fiddle in a Hee-Haw band." As she sits back in her seat, she realizes that she allowed her ego and insecurities to be exposed. She knows this puts relationships on the line, including the one with Channing, and makes her look like an insecure asshole in the process. A deafening silence falls between the two women. Channing pays for lunch and they both go back to the office.

Eighteen months later, their vice-president announces that he accepted another position; his successor—a woman—has been identified. The successor is...

Although women in the workforce have come a long way, a very small percentage of women exist in top executive positions within Fortune 500 companies. Some corporations have diversity goals and, when prompted or encouraged to promote women, they unconsciously plant the "there can be only one" seed. While observing the reaction among those women who seek the few executive positions, a very clear distinction between the "Absolute 8" Alphas and the others appears.

The "Absolute 8" female understands her position, caliber, skills, talents, options, and environment. She strategizes her moves against her competition, but is not intimidated by them. When one Alpha Female recognizes another, she shows respect to the other, and they either create a lasting relationship, or connect in such a way that there is mutual respect and the leveraging of each other's skills. Conversely, non-Alpha Females or "Augmented 8" Alphas allow for their insecurities or egos to get in the way easier, bringing forth the high probability of feeling intimidated or threatened. This creates a "survival" mode.

When the "there can be only one" scenario presents itself between "Absolute" and "non-Absolute" Alpha Females, outside manipulation easily creates high levels of friction, heighten insecurities, and cut-throat tactics that produce detrimental no-win results.

The same scenario between two "Absolute" Alpha Females executes differently. The two females first recognize the other for who she is and respect her space; almost like an unspoken bond. If they clash, it's exposed through competition. They step up their game, maintain a keen awareness of external forces, and honor the "let the best Alpha Female win" approach.

An alternative approach with two "Absolute" Alphas creates the collusion affect where they align to create a "you scratch my back, I scratch yours" solution. They strategize, exploit the external forces presented, and create the stealthy collusion so that one of the Alphas gains the upper position, leveraging it to pull the other Alpha upward; thereby, disproving the "there can be only one" myth.

Corporate Seductress or Corporate Seduced? Part 2

After successfully executing various roles across the company, Channing returns to the original business where she began her career. She now plays with the corporate big boys on their field. She carries the torch of being the only woman on the executive team. Although her peers respect her abilities, many worked extensively to hinder her progression, tarnish her reputation, and support the "lynch the bitch" campaign. The intentional roadblocks and traps were humbling awakenings for Channing. Through influential maneuvering and securing support from key board members, peers, and corporate executives, Channing persevered; obtaining the goal she sought.

Every day, Channing plays the games of the male-dominated industry with the mindset of men and the sensuality of women, having her acknowledged as a boss, but not bossy, and a bitch, but not bitchy—or so she believes. The authoritative, financial, and social power intoxicates Channing as it would a man. She enjoys mentoring and coaching the younger employees' careers to success. She creates special teams with these young employees to work on major company initiatives. These teams report directly to her. Her beauty, status, youth, and style draw the women to admire her and the men to fanaticize about her.

Within each class, Channing selects an employee to guide and mentor more intimately. The special selection consists mostly of male employees. The five-to eight-year age difference between Channing and the team creates a comfort level that allows the men to flirt with her and attempt to pursue her socially. The ones specially selected believe they position themselves to seduce her, creating a romantic liaison. Channing, fully aware of their intentions, allows the game to run its course. She accepts working dinners, yet cancels due to her schedule, heightening their interests. She eventually creates the environment in which they'll "seduce her." The initial encounter takes the younger men from excited anticipation to unbridled ecstasy. Channing enjoys their eagerness to please her in both the boardroom and bedroom, but ensures they understand that complete discretion and confidentiality is mandatory. The guys, exhibiting bold egos, believe they powerfully seduced the boss, created an inside advantage to bolster their careers, and secured a special place within her soul and bed. During the relationship, the guys experience the "ride" of their lives, as she creates the illusion of they are her only relationship and her best *lover. She creates experiences that would make the creators of "Fifty Shades of Grey" blush. Her power strengthens with each encounter. Channing continues to feed their egos by leveraging assignments they find as opportunities and ensuring performance recognition/rewards. The guys think to themselves, "What could be better? I am the man," until their season with Channing dwindles to an end. When Channing decides it's time for the relationship to end, she presents the dissolution as, "you need to grow your career," "my schedule is too busy," "there's no time for a serious relationship." Then, she promotes them to a remote location. The guys receive gained opportunities, handsome performance bonuses, and are made to believe they controlled the deal. She ensures the other team members progress positively, challenge themselves, and move to career-growing positions to eliminate the perception of favoritism. The employees participating on her special teams love working for her. Channing, reveling at her power, cleanses herself of the tryst until the next season. All parties received a benefit, so no harm, no foul, right? Well…*

Was Channing the seducer or the one being seduced?

Alpha Females, especially those performing in the same environments and roles as Alpha Males, have the same power, desires, egos and leverages as their male counterparts. The late Oscar Wilde once stated: "Everything in the world is about sex, except sex. Sex is about power." The statement rings no truer than in the world of the Alpha, male or female. Elevated intellect, libido, and positional power create the ultimate aphrodisiac. Although most Alpha Females would not cross the professional line in the aforementioned manner *(as with the idiom "They will not shit where they eat.")*, it is not uncommon for them to create a varied scenario of power that could be misconstrued, representative of a succubus.

This scenario highlights the ability of the Alpha Female to create the illusion of control and seduction belonging to the male participant. Most of them are unaware that they were selected, targeted, and controlled throughout the experience. They believe they accomplished the "art of seduction" to gain an advantage or obtain what they want; thereby controlling the situation. Yet, the real power lies with the Alpha Female. Her ability to create the illusion is independent of the sex variable. The multiple strings of power created by Alpha Females bring about a desired, long-lasting intimate connection with an ever present "ace in the hole" card to be utilized at her leisure. If and when the male realizes he was the one seduced, the internal questioning if his rewards were more boardroom or bedroom performance-based creates a level of insecurity and vulnerability for exploitation. The same type of "seduction" occurs with a female target—not sexually—but the same connection and rewarding illusion create the strings that lead to the "ace in the hole" just the same.

As the thought, "Damn, ruthless bitch" or worse enters your mind, ask yourself: Would the same thought occur if the seductor in this scenario was an Alpha Male? Society quickly casts the negative double standard judgment on her for the same strategic movements that lead to positive successes or questionable infractions exhibited by her male counterparts. When is the double standard of judgment extinguished?

Boardroom Boss or Ultimate Bitch?

A few years after leading her special team program, Channing's performance continues to exceed expectations with the executive board members. Although rumors surface about her previous attention to her "special recruits," the corporate wagons quickly circled to dispel them, protecting Channing. She believes the board fully supports and advocates for her, along with her executive peers.

During the quarterly board meeting, an announcement comes forth that the reigning COO will retire within the next twelve months. The top three successor candidates are announced; Channing is one of them. Continuing her trailblazing successes, she is the youngest and only female of the three candidates. She beams with excitement for an opportunity to execute the next phase of her career. Channing, quickly surveying the environment, initiates her plan for securing the position with the board. Her focus tightens on some key board members and her main adversary, a fellow candidate named Barrett. She knows the corporate game well, has maneuvered through the minutia while obtaining bumps and bruises along the way, and believes her ability to produce and seduce makes her the top contender.

The candidates understand they are being assessed now more than ever by the company, and any hint of risk to causing instability with shareholders seals their fate of elimination. Channing, keenly astute of her environment, notices small adjustments of meeting invites, social events, and her scope of responsibilities. She discovers a major "lynch the bitch" campaign, targeting her, and suspects her main adversary leads the campaign. Over the next six months, Channing works to showcase her abilities of creating shareholder value and mitigate any risks that may create doubt in the minds of the board. There are many questionable behaviors leaked to the board involving Channing. The behaviors range from creative financial reporting to rumored inappropriate relationships with other employees, which could raise questions on her competency as well. She notices her charms lessening with the board and the tide shifting away from her favor. The leaked information maintained rumored form, but created a stable doubt with the board. She experiences continual lack of support as each week passes, causing her concern for the ability to maintain her executive position. She calmly formulates her next set of moves to defend her position and create the offense to flush out the lynching leader. Within the next three months, her seductive hold has been reduced to less than a finger grip of reality, while the other candidates appear to be favored.

The last thirty days of the twelve-month window exerts major pressure on Channing. As the announcement of the next COO approaches, tensions of executive positioning mounts and the campaign against Channing neutralizes her maneuverability; but, the company continues to keep her as a contender to mitigate allegations of discrimination. However, there is a plan to announce the removal of Channing, due to corporate infractions, the day of the new COO announcement.

Announcement day arrives presenting Barrett as the new COO, who confirms to Channing his seduction of instituting her lynching campaign. Channing congratulates him with her "smile-fuck" grin and a mob boss-style hug, creating an instant gasp of breath in Barrett, as if it would be his last. Channing quickly makes an announcement: She resigned from her position, as of the zero hour of that very morning, to assume her new role as CEO of their top competitor. She thanks everyone for their support and years of service and exits the building. A deafening silence fills the room as Channing not only nixes her public execution, but maneuvers herself to a larger role with a competitor—where she brings all of the known disadvantages of her former employer. Before the day ends, she manages to seduce a few, trusted, diverse executives to join her at the competitor company, thus creating major turmoil at the previous company, as well as creating confidence instability with their newly announced COO.

Barrett, befriending Channing for years, worries about the competitive storm brewing. His knowledge of Channing's strengths and her ability to toil with, torture, and crucify her competition, keeps him up at night—every night.

Did Channing get what she deserved?

Alpha Females, especially those who wear their egos like expensive trench coats, risk being seduced by their own seduction. The risk clouds their awareness that "the game you play will eventually play you," allowing others to leverage their blind-spots. There are rare occasions when they are completely caught off guard; but, their ability to adjust quickly and utilize well-guarded bypass tunnels and exit strategies allows them to maneuver and regain balance.

An Alpha Female expects full loyalty from anyone she lets into her limited inner circle. Once a member breaks the loyalty, the penalty is held in perpetuity. The Alpha Female imposes the penalty of her choice at her leisure, leaving the offensive member scared shitless.

There have been some Alpha Females temporarily eliminated by the "lynch the bitch" campaigns in the corporate world. She can get comfortable with her own power, or perceived power, and with corporate feeding the power by using the bait of more. People, especially men, scratch their heads and wonder "How did she know?" and "How did she escape the traps and extermination?"

Corporate America tries to neutralize her, attempts to crucify her, and many times denies her, believing the Alpha Female can be eliminated. This belief brings grave damage and figurative fatal results. Just when a person believes she has no clue to the political schemes unfolding, she does. She does not disclose, as to observe the movements of the players and uncover if the inner circle was breeched. Once she recognizes the ring leader and the henchmen, they are mentally compartmentalized and placed on the Alpha Female's "hit list." She steps up the influence with her network, waits for the right opportunity to expose the Judas, and creates a threatening position of power. She carries out her "hit list" by calculating the right scenarios at the right time with the right people, and ensuring her bidding executes precisely with no traceability to her (unless she decides to disclose). All in the name of seduction: The Ultimate Boardroom Boss.

CHAPTER FOUR

Dating: "A" Game Or Game Over

While interviewing men about dating the Alpha Female, a common theme presented itself; many believed they had dated one at some point and could easily recognize an Alpha Female. Speaking with them in more depth, reality exposed the opposite of both beliefs. These misguided beliefs persuade men's attitude and perception when they actually encounter an Alpha Female in a social setting, and leads to them being misguided in their approach and further relationship building. Many men have asked, "How do I approach an authentic Alpha Female and keep her interested enough to date me?"

One driving belief embedded in the psyche of the Alpha Female is summed up in this quote by Oscar Wilde: "I have the simplest of tastes. I am always satisfied with the best." This belief manifests itself in every aspect of her life, including the dating scene. It is an elevated standard, embodied by the belief that raises the aforementioned question by men. The Alpha Female is very approachable in a social setting; however, when approached, the male must not make the mistake of executing the one-size-fits-all, stale pick-up line; this effort will be futile. While his "A" game may entice most women, it will be considered too ordinary and average by an Alpha Female. These women know what they like and don't entertain the bullshit. They are easily turned off. However, even they can get into sticky relationships; the traits that draw men to them ultimately can create distain and contempt by men toward them.

Discussions over Drinks

CJ and a few of her comrades, given their hectic schedules, decide to catch up over cocktails at a popular happy hour place for professionals. There she meets up with Tristen, Cerena, and Sloane. CJ is last to arrive; she scans the rooms as she makes her entrance, takes note of her surroundings, and joins the other ladies at their table. She offers to pay for the first round of cocktails and the ladies settle into the happy hour scene. After discussing their work week, the conversation soon turns to their social lives. They notice nice-looking guys at another table, whom they know have noticed them. They get into the discussion of "dating worthiness."

The guys have gathered at this happy hour to catch up as well. They are corporate men, much like the ladies, who want to unwind. The gentlemen — Kaden, Drew, Tony, and Sean — notice the ladies, and become engaged in their own conversation on women, types of women, and "dating worthiness." Tony knows Cerena through a mutual friend, but only in passing, which he mentions to the others as they comment on how nice these ladies represent themselves. Drew informs Tony that he is interested in meeting Cerena. Tony warns him that Cerena is not the typical female that he is used to dating, and mentions he has witnessed Cerena shutting down other "playas" previously. Drew assures the guys that he will not be shot down. Kaden (whom CJ observed when she entered the room) notices CJ; he decided he would ask her out before the night ends.

The ladies proceed to the outdoor patio and sit near the patio fireplace. CJ decides it is time for another round of cocktails; she goes inside to the bar and orders another round for her and the ladies. She knows this gives Kaden (or another suitor) the opportunity to approach her, if he chooses. Kaden, keeping a distant watch, takes the opportunity to make his way to the bar and introduces himself to CJ. She acknowledges his introduction, but seems unimpressed. He offers to buy her a drink. She politely declines. CJ decides to buy him and his boys a round of drinks, pays for them, and makes her way back to the patio, disclosing the event to the girls. They chuckle at the lame approach as the men come out to the patio to thank CJ and gain permission to join the ladies around the fireplace. Tony and Cerena politely say hello, acknowledging that they had met previously. They compare notes on the internal conversations of each group to realize they were having the same type of discussion: Dating...and the worthiness of him/her. The men are so impressed by CJ's gesture that they offer to pay for the next round of cocktails. (The ladies did not have to pay for drinks for the remainder of the night.) The guys continue the worthiness discussion with the women on dating the "strong, Alpha-type" woman and share their views. Tony and Sean believe these types women are like cacti, beautiful but prickly to the touch. They remark that these women types do not want to be treated like fragile ladies in the boardroom but expect to be treated with door-opening treatment outside the office. They make reference to these women not willing to "let a man be a man" in household duties or on the job. Although they claim to admire these ladies for their business savvy and agree that they live in a man's world, they remark that they feel that they can be less-feminine because they are less submissive and perceived as "too" strong. CJ and Cerena give each other an "Are they serious?" look. Drew and Kaden, being interested in Cerena and CJ respectively, smirk while Tony and Sean continue expressing their views on the dating-worthy women. They remark that they like women who are smart and make their own money, but still know their roles as women. Sean mentions that most women are happy when a man approaches and offers to buy them a drink, while some of the more independent women feel it is an insult. He cannot understand why they feel they need to show they have balls. He expresses (with Tony agreeing) the affinity for women that he considers feminine, who understand their roles and are approachable. He says a woman should, for example, let a man change her car's oil or get it changed for her; she doesn't need to do everything herself. They express that Tristen and Sloane seem more of the approachable description. Tristen and Sloane are somewhat irritated, yet the "compliments" from Tony and Sean make them more open to understanding, as they believe the guys revel in their femininity, and the ladies concur with some of their views. Cerena peers at Tony with distain. CJ and Cerena decide to voice their views on dating worthiness.

CJ and Cerena acknowledge the views of Sean and Tony. The ladies give their views of the men they find worth dating. They want a true Alpha Male that has his own busy schedule, exudes high confidence—not arrogance—embraces their female counterparts, is a compliment to them as a power couple, shines in *corporate and social settings, and is able to adapt from a corporate event to go-cart racing if the feeling hits. They make it clear they want a man to be a man, but he has to be able to handle the masculine energy as expected. They would greatly appreciate their man changing the oil in their car. However, if they need to travel on Wednesday, they inform him they need it done by Tuesday. When Tuesday arrives the guy is still sitting on the couch in his boxers with one hand on the remote and one in their boxers with no oil change in sight, WHICH is what they have issues with. "If they want to be the man, then take care of business like a man," remarks Cerena. They are not looking for men that need to be nurtured, mothered, or are emotionally high-maintenance. CJ pipes up, "He cannot get upset if I kick his butt in the weekly football pool." Cerena nods in agreement. Cerena highlights criteria of not being intimidated by her paycheck, confidence, decision-making skills, or assertiveness. She smirks at Tony, remarking the initial criteria would be the "anti-Tony." She notes that Tony and Sean may be used to dating "fake Fendis."*

Kaden and Drew, along with the rest, chuckle at the anti-Tony crack. Drew calmly expresses his views of the fact that he fits the criteria Cerena mentioned, and he has dated some "A-type" women in the past. He says that he does not fully agree with his friends' expressed views; rather, he embraces and highly respects these women types and does not find them less feminine than others. He coyly hints that Cerena is just his type, that he likes her look, her style, and how she handles herself in a social setting.

65

Kaden calmly suggests another round of cocktails and invites CJ to walk with him to the bar. CJ gives him a quick ten second seductive stare, rises from her seat, and joins Kaden. As they walk to the bar, Kaden strikes up a conversation with CJ about her day, his day, social affairs, business activities, and leisure interests. He successfully deters the conversation from the previous debate of the sexes. CJ compliments him on his deterring moves, letting him know that she was not fooled by the dissuasion. He praises her keen observance. They do the "I noticed you noticing me" dance for a few minutes until the order was completed. Kaden inquires about openings on her schedule so they can have a more in-depth, private conversation. He obtains CJ's number, informing her he would like to invite her on a date. As they return to meet the others on the patio, they discover an elevated discussion on "dating worthiness likes and dislikes."

Tony brings up his issue with the "90-day rule" of women, remarking this was a plot of controlling men from a popular book and movie. He asks the group if they believe in the "90-day rule." Sloan answers that, while she may not count the days, she believes there should be a period of getting to know someone, she does not believe in one night stands, and men should respect a woman's ruleset no matter the rules. Cerena informs him that real women, especially women such as herself, have no hard and fast rules; she is much like the Alpha Male, if she sees something she wants, she may choose to conquer with no other additional commitment or contact in mind. She exhibits the ability to separate emotions from sex when most men want more from her. She challenges Tony on his character for even broaching the subject as criteria for dating worthiness and his choice of women to date. Then, she challenges him on his earlier comments about women wanting to be more like men and, if they are in the case of the 90-day rule, why does he have such a double standard?

Tony, stunned by her candid comments and movements, goes silent. Sean attempts to come to his rescue by challenging her morals. Tristen, slightly irritated, challenges Sean on the double standard of expectations of serial or parallel dating by women versus men. Why does he feel men should play the field and women cannot? Why should a woman suppress her high libido, where a man should be glorified for it? The men really have no rebuttal, except to offer the perception of being viewed as a lady or a whore, which douses fuel on a fiery conversation. CJ takes an attorney's approach in stating that Sean and Tony want a feminine, virtuous woman—but only for fewer than 90 days—who should not date multiple men at the same time (even if she is not engaged in sexual relations with them); yet, they want a freak in the bedroom and a money-maker who doesn't outshine them. Once CJ lays out the transcript of what the men conveyed, everyone goes silent. The guys have painted themselves in a corner as they realize their next move could derail any chances with Tristen and Sloane. Before they can respond, CJ saves them by commenting on her busy schedule, calling it a night. Kaden walks CJ to her vehicle, laughing at the events of the night. CJ asks why he found it humorous. She didn't. He quickly adjusts to a serious look, agreeing his buddies should have better embracement of all women. CJ looks at him with a *"don't bullshit me" stare for a few seconds then gives him a quick smirk-like grin. Kaden informs CJ he will call her for a date. CJ eases into her luxury sports vehicle and peels off into the night.*

Drew gathers the courage to ask Cerena for her number. Cerena says she does not believe it is a good idea, in light of the night's conversations. She believes that Drew has many of the same views and beliefs as his buddies. Drew challenges her not to lump all men together just as she does not want to be lumped in a category. He tries to assure Cerena his friends' views in no way represent him. Cerena hesitantly gives him her number, walks out of the venue and heads home.

Tony and Sean continue to converse with Tristen and Sloane for a few more ticks of the clock, until the ladies decide to it's time to leave. They exchange information and agree they would like to continue the dialog and have some fun.

When it comes to an initial social setting and approaching an Alpha Female, most men believe they understand how to approach her, but many are highly mistaken. If they approach with standard one-liners, they will barely be acknowledged, much less get a response. Alpha Females are always aware of their surroundings. In any social setting, they will have done a quick scan of the scene upon arrival. They do not worry about who may be scoping them. When approaching an Alpha Female at a social event, like a happy hour, dinner party, charity event, or elite society gala, it is best to observe her before approaching. Simply asking if you can buy her a drink is not impressive, whether or not she accepts. However, not offering, based on respect her for who she is, may be viewed as disrespectful or cheap. More than likely, she will offer to buy him a drink to ensure he understands she is not tied to him nor that she "owes" him anything. This also signifies that she does not need him to buy her drink; she can match him glass for glass. If she is at a table with her crew, upon approach you must show the crew respect by acknowledging them as well. To gain her attention, buy drinks for the crew (typically two to four people), signifying confidence and gentlemanly character.

If a man perceives that the "player approach" may work, he should remember that she likely has more than one on her roster and may embrace serial or parallel dating until she finds those select few who are worthy of her time or commitment of exclusivity. She quickly compartmentalizes the dating worthiness of the man who approaches her by his intellect, execution of a non-conventional approach, the confidence-versus-arrogance factor, subtle movements, and choice of words. Her standards are above the rest, so men must bring their "A" game—or stay home.

The First Date

Kaden calls CJ two days later, leaving her a voicemail, and requests a date to get to know her better. Meanwhile, Drew has called Cerena to invite her to a movie.

Later in the evening, CJ returns Kaden's call and agrees to a date. She informs him of her congested schedule, but would still like to go out with him. He sets a dinner date for the upcoming Friday night. As Friday draws closer, CJ has a work conflict and reschedules for the following Thursday night, because she has a flight on Friday morning. Kaden confirms the schedule adjustment. Kaden remembers the conversation they had from the happy hour event that included some discussions of their likes and favorite things when it comes to food and fun. They agree to meet at one of the high-end restaurants which they both favor. When CJ arrives at the luxurious bistro, she is met by a dedicated maître d who shows her to the table, pulls out her chair, and checks her personal items, showing her the red carpet treatment. She realizes there is no one there but her and wonders if she was early or had the correct date. As the staff greets her with her favorite wine, Kaden approaches, dressed to impress, with the well-known chef beside him to greet CJ. He has the entire restaurant booked for the two of them to ensure they have a classy, private, uninterrupted dinner to get to know each other better. (He has close ties with the owner and chef.) The chef and staff are there to create the meal of her choice; they have the option for live music, if she chooses. Kaden informs CJ that this night belongs to her.

CJ smiles, showing she is pleased but not yet sure if she is impressed, and places her order with the chef. She and Kaden converse about everything from politics, careers, hobbies, sports, social events, and share a quick peek into their personal lives. CJ ensures she gains more insight on Kaden than he can with her, keeping her psychological edge. He takes CJ on a personal tour of the exquisite wine cellar that is hidden from most guests. As they converse over a customized five-course meal, they find they have many things in common, including a major vice for watches. They notice each other's movements, responses, body language, and overall taste. Time seemed to fly in seconds rather than hours. CJ peers at her watch, reminds Kaden of her early flight the next morning, and thanks him for a great evening. As the maître d brings her personal items, Kaden stops her for one last item. The chef presents her with a parting gift, an autographed bottle of one of the most expensive wines—it's one of her favorites. The valet has her vehicle waiting as Kaden walks her to it, ensures she enters safely and sensually kisses her cheek and whispers "Call me when you arrive home." The two part ways and CJ heads home to prepare for her flight and meeting the next day.

Cerena accepts Drew's invitation to a movie, with the option for light cocktails or dinner to follow. Cerena has a few reservations about Drew as she believes he is not used to dating women like her, although he has claimed differently. She likes meeting new people and the outing is nothing more than that chance. Cerena recalls that Drew is very handsome and has a great body.

She and Drew meet at the entrance of the movie theater. As Cerena walks toward the entrance, she sees Drew dressed in stylish pullover sweater and jeans. He greets her with a red rose as he opens the door. She accepts the flower to not hurt his feelings, but thinks to herself, "Really?" He pays for their snacks and they enter the cinema. During the movie, Drew tries to make some small talk and puts his arm behind her on the chair as he leans in. After the movie, they visit a local restaurant/bar for appetizers and cocktails. They converse mostly on social issues, life revelations, hobbies, and some career topics. Cerena leads the conversation more toward finding out what drives and influences Drew. She notices that he seems to be working hard to impress her, which she finds complementary, although he really has not succeeded. After about ninety minutes of conversation, Cerena decides to call it a night. She insists on paying for the food and drinks, which impresses Drew. He walks Cerena to her vehicle, where she gives him a hug, thanks him for a good outing, and heads home. Drew leaves believing he was "the man" on the date and feels very content.

The next day at work, Cerena receives three dozen long-stem roses with expensive imported chocolates. Her executive assistant accepts the delivery and walks it to Cerena's office. Those in the office are impressed by the gift. Upon arrival, and much to her assistant's surprise, Cerena requires the gift be put in the break room or in the open area to dress it up, but not in her office. She receives a text soon after inquiring if she received the delivery. She replies with a simple "Yes."

Later that evening Drew calls Cerena to hear about her day at work (actually hoping to hear how she and the team were impressed by his gift). During the call, he notices that Cerena did not mention the delivery, so he inquires on her thoughts. She politely informs him that she really does not care for flowers or candy. Drew seems stunned; that gesture usually earns him major kudos with the other women. Cerena, understanding Drew really does not get it, invites him to a popular college football game. Drew, who played college ball, readily agrees. He welcomes another chance to make an impression on Cerena. In this case, they decide to redo the first date.

Cerena meets Drew at the college stadium. He thinks to himself, "What could be better than an intelligent, good-looking, woman who loves football?" As they walk toward the entrance, Drew reaches for the door to go to general admission, when Cerena stops him and motions to follow her as she opens the door for VIP admission to the skybox area. She has the passes, tickets, and other perks in store. Drew looks at her for a quick second to ensure she is not teasing him as he walks through the door with a huge grin. They take the elevator to the skybox where the venue is fully catered with an open bar, luxuriously seated, and includes some heavy hitters in the social scene, not to mention a celebrity or two. Cerena is greeted as soon as they enter with many looking to gain a moment of her time. She makes her way around the room, advises Drew to get comfortable to have a great time. Drew realizes he has encountered a different caliber of woman, so he needs to step up his game. Cerena engages him throughout the game and continues to work the room; the event is social, business, and fun for her all in one. She introduces Drew to a few people. By the ending whistle, Drew left the venue having more fun than he could have imagined. He becomes more intrigued, impressed, and infatuated with Cerena's poise, look, presence, style, and class. He believes that she really could be the one for him. Cerena tells Drew she hopes he enjoyed himself and that she has a busy week with meetings for which she needs to prepare. While Drew understands, he does not *want the day to end. He promises to call her during the week. When Cerena receives his text before the next morning, it's clear to her that she set the desired expectation point for Drew. Now, she needs to see if he steps up or steps off.*

The Alpha Female does not believe in or appreciate clichés. Although many men believe they have met, approached, and dated Alpha Females, their answers to "What do you do for a first date?" reveals the false nature of their belief. These women not only have busy schedules and complex lives, they also influence the situation to meet their agenda. Oftentimes, they maneuver the day, time, and location of the date either due to their schedules or simply because they have the power to do it.

One common theme with the majority of Alpha Females is "No flowers!" (or candy) on a first date. Why? Because they die. Flowers are impractical and require maintenance, her schedule is busy enough, and they are cliché for a first date. Men, if you should not approach her with a cliché pick-up line, what makes you believe you could have a cliché first—or subsequent—date? The best approach is to pay attention to what she likes and dislikes, and to step it up in a non-conventional way.

The Alpha Female is not easily impressed. She is paying close attention to the style, taste, and class of the men to whom she gives her precious time. The best approach is to find out about her or pay attention to what she likes and dislikes and step it up in a non-conventional way.

Many times she will "pick up the tab," especially if she is not impressed or enjoying the date, to ensure the guy knows she owes him nothing and is free to walk away anytime. She easily recognizes the difference between a heart-felt compliment or a remark made to feed her ego. If you want to capture her attention, and keep it to build a relationship, you must ensure she experiences the same treatment of grace and style to which she is accustomed. Don't mistake the Alpha Female for being a "Miss Priss." She is exactly the opposite; she is not prissy and doesn't mind getting "down and dirty;" yet, her version is executed with graced style. She is classy, keeps her femininity, and walks away without compromise. If you try to impress her she becomes less impressed. Impress her with what comes naturally. She embraces real men; those without drama, who do not instigate trouble, and are not emotionally high-maintenance. If a man exhibits he is one Midol and half a menstrual cramp away from being female, she shuts it down immediately. She is turned off by bitchy men.

When it comes to first date gifts, give her something classy that she can actually use. Pay attention to what is important to her; like an autographed bottle of her favorite wine, a favorite team shirt, or something personal for her office, so she thinks of you when she uses it.

Whether the first date encompasses a sporting event, movie, dinner, or other type of outing, she can adapt to any situation but she will not *settle* for any situation. Men, please note: To get her to be interested in a second date, you must be very perceptive on the first date.

Relationships: Intense Passion or Passion to Posses

Despite having a lack-luster first date, Drew and Cerena form a more intimate relationship. Drew becomes more aware of the caliber of woman he is pursing. He realizes Cerena does not fit the mold of the women he once dated, as Tony remarked at the happy hour. Although he shows confidence to an almost-arrogant state at times, deep down he wonders if he can keep up with her. He becomes not only intrigued, but also infatuated with the characteristics he believes makes her the perfect woman for him: non-clingy, non-possessive, loves sports, able to chill out with the guys, competitive, fit, financially independent, responsible, moves with womanly poise, and exhibits an intense libido. Cerena observes Drew's feelings for her and notices his willingness to become more of the man he believes she desires.

CJ and Kaden continue to build upon their great first date. Kaden, who has a schedule as congested as CJ's, continues to keep CJ interested in him. He and CJ are alike in career levels, schedules, lifestyles, views, taste, egos, and libidos. The dual Alpha-ism creates a seductive "push/pull" that neither can resist. They understand and respect each other's space and time. They continue to have mind-blowing rendezvous to make up for the gaps of time in between. They are on the verge of the "exclusivity" discussion, which both know could be a challenge for the other. They are having fun; they work hard and play harder.

During the first six months of Drew and Cerena's relationship, it seems relatively smooth. Cerena received another promotion which requires more travel, both domestic and international. In the beginning, Drew appeared supportive; however, Cerena started to notice a few comments from him questioning her feelings for him, her schedule, and who she met for business. Cerena gives him the reassurance he needs, but also reminds him of the woman she is. She makes it clear if he does not feel comfortable with the relationship, she has no reservation on parting ways. Drew assures her of his confidence and internal security.

Around the year anniversary of them dating, Cerena and Drew attend one of her company's socials. Cerena, as usual, receives attention from many of her colleague and executive leadership, most of them men. Although she introduces Drew as the man in her life, she notices his change in demeanor. (She thinks it strange being that, when she attends his company's events, he attracts attention from the women and Cerena does not feel threatened.) Cerena and Drew attend the event for another hour, then head to her place. Drew stays fairly silent during the ride. Once there, he brings up the idea of moving in together; Cerena feels as if she is not ready for that level of commitment. Drew moved within a five-mile radius to where Cerena lives. The response draws significant anger from Drew; he starts accusing her of infidelity, flirting, pulling away

77

from him, and being elusive. They start to argue and he quickly pins her against the wall with his forearm across her chest, while yelling obscenities. Cerena stays calm, demanding that he release her immediately. Drew quickly comes to his senses, releases her, but can see that he has completely crossed the line with Cerena. He starts to apologize for behaving poorly all evening, but Cerena demands that he leave. Cerena sits quietly for a moment, then calls one of her closest friends, CJ. Because CJ lives by the Alpha Female and friendship codes, she knows she can trust her with anything.

CJ arrives with haste, bottles of wine in hand. She finds Cerena sitting quietly in her home with a look of deep disappointment and slight agitation. She tells CJ the entire story, with one tear she allows to stream down her face. CJ actively listens while empathizing with her. CJ asks if this was his first act of violence. Cerena nods. CJ tells Cerena that a few of the girls had noticed Drew's behavior on occasion and became concerned, but they did not want to butt in. She informs her there were whispers of how he treated other women he dated; as if they were second-class citizens, wanting them to cater to him, and most of them obliged. When they no longer wanted that arrangement, he would become a different person. From there, she comforts Cerena by listening, and gives her some sisterly advice: first, pay attention to the signs, and second, Drew may not be the man that he claims to be.

They drink more wine and discuss intimate experiences with past relationships. CJ suggests that Cerena may need to consider an order of protection from Drew. Cerena says the thought crossed her mind, but this may have been a one-time incident, as he knows she does not tolerate the behavior. CJ gives her a hug, tells her to stay safe and, if she needs anything, to not hesitate to call her.

CJ and Kaden's relationship continues to flourish. Their challenges centers on the areas that attract them to each other. They have limited time on their schedule, but when they are together they have a great time; and, sex in any room is never a problem for them—the more intense the better. They also understand that the business travel and their typical natures make being monogamous, in a non-determined exclusive relationship, a slim probability. During one evening at Kaden's home, he mentions exclusivity to CJ. CJ is somewhat shocked that Kaden initiates the discussion, but smiles at him and says that she would be open to being exclusive. She requires that he define what "exclusive" means to him to ensure they are on the same expectation page. Kaden responds with they would be an official couple rather than the top of each other's dating roster; he expresses expectation of "monogamy." He confesses to her about the deeper, intimate feelings he has for her. CJ chuckles for a moment, understanding exactly what he means, then agrees to exclusivity with Kaden. They laugh, and then enjoy a steamy night in his indoor hot tub. The next morning, they take separate flights to out-of-town meetings.

After the "incident," Drew tries to offer his deepest apologies to Cerena, but she denies his calls. Drew invites her to dinner a number of times, but she declines. One evening, Cerena has dinner with a male friend from high school, whom she had not seen in years. They enjoy an innocent dinner with lots of laughs about the good ol' days. As they were walking to Cerena's car, Drew appears.

She did not know that he had been watching her every move. He starts a scene in the parking lot about who she was with and if that was his replacement. Ethan attempts to calm Drew on the fact he and Cerena are only friends, but Cerena asks Ethan to leave, as she has the situation under control. Drew starts such a brash scene, Cerena's friend, Ethan, doubles back to check on her. Ethan gets out of his car to ask Cerena if she is okay; Drew cusses at him to mind his own business. Before Cerena could blink, Drew punches Ethan and a scuffle ensues. The police are called and Drew is arrested for assault. Drew posts bond by the end of the night and immediately goes to Cerena's home to beg her to let him explain. She denies him entry to her home, but he stands outside her door expressing that no woman made him feel the way she does: he loves her style, confidence, personality, and how she helps him be better in life. He claims she was the woman for him. Cerena promises to call the police if he does not leave her property. He finally leaves, but promises that he will win her over.

Over the next few months Drew calls, texts, sends messages and gifts to Cerena's place of employment, and follows all of her movements. He shows up on her doorstep at the weirdest times. Cerena files an order of protection and informs Drew that they were no longer going to affiliate; he should move on and find another woman to his liking. Drew, unwilling to accept Cerena's decision, decides that he is going to make her listen and want him again.

One morning as she was leaving for work, Drew approaches her at the entry and pushes his way inside her home, armed with a hunting knife and gun. He informs her that she needs to listen to him and then she would understand and give him another chance. Cerena tries to stay calm as Drew informs her that if she does not, neither of them are leaving the home again; meaning he would kill her and then himself. She asks him to explain why he was fixated on her, while silently praying for a way out of the situation with her life intact. Drew starts to reminisce on when he first saw her at the happy hour and noticed that she was not like many of the other women he encountered. He informs her he always admired her way around people, her intelligence, her body, her strength, her successes, and the fact people seemed to genuinely respect and like her. He informs her that she was the best sexual experience he ever had, and that he could not stand to lose her and her attributes to another man. The things she had, he wanted and wanted for himself only.

By this time, a few hours had passed and her co-workers noticed that she was not at work. Her phone was going to voicemail. They knew of the Drew situation, so they decided to call the police to go to her home. They felt she could be in trouble. Drew continues to try to convince Cerena why they should be together. She realizes that what pulled Drew to her are the same things he wants to control; when he could not, it turned into hate. He loved to hate her underneath it all. Drew blames her for not "submitting" herself and allowing him to be "the man" he had always been. Drew goes from rage to tears, while Cerena tries to keep him calm and encourage him to leave. The police arrive to a hostage-style crisis. Drew vows that before the police would arrest him, he would take Cerena's and his own lives.

The incident becomes breaking news. Kaden and CJ arrive at the home and Kaden tries to convince Drew to come outside unarmed. Kaden cannot believe Drew has snapped. Kaden realizes from CJ's reaction that something has been brewing, but CJ always kept her confidentiality with her close friends.

SWAT arrived and within less than thirty minutes, it was all over. They were able to get sites on Drew and kill him with one shot. They acted in time, as Drew was close enough to Cerena to harm her with the hunting knife. She saw his body hit the floor, with his brains leaking next to him. She got out of the chair where she had been cornered for hours and walked out in shock. The police and emergency response stormed her home, while CJ and Kaden were there to comfort her in her vulnerable time of need. She had never been so vulnerable in her life; there was not a description that could fully capture her state at that moment.

Six months later, Kaden asks CJ to be engaged to him. CJ had already informed Kaden that she did not want to be married as she never wanted to be a "wife," and he agreed that he never wanted to be a "husband." They both agreed that marriage brought about additional expectations, and they were both fine with being engaged. The "Oprah-Stedman" type of relationship works for them.

Cerena had moved into a new home and was beginning to date again.

The dating Alpha Female accepts the challenge that what many men find attractive in her can also cause them to eventually resent and/or hate her. These ladies usually pair well with authentic Alpha Males, who likely understand them the most. But, the matchup comes with a price. The mirrored image can also create a "magnetic attraction and magnetic repelling" effect; a constant positive and sexual tension. The gamble is that a "competitive" nature can interfere with what brought them together initially. The roster of dating options, high libidos, and attention from the opposite sex as they work their schedules, always presents a challenge to the issue of monogamy. When they are "monogamous," it may present itself in an unconventional manner (to be discussed later).

This is not to say that non-Alphas could or should not date an Alpha Female. The non-Alpha would have to be very secure within his skin to be able to relate to and embrace her. The challenge that happens with non-Alphas is the "Love to Hate" scenario. The example of Cerena and Drew is an extreme case; however, many times the characteristics that draw these men are the very characteristics they eventually grow to resent; either because they do not possess these characteristics themselves, or they cannot control the characteristics within her. She is who she is, whether or not in a relationship. Many men expect a more docile or submissive change, which never happens. There have been stories disclosed where the men in these ladies' lives were drawn to them for who they were, but have had stalking, controlling, or envy issues once they feel they have to compete with her. These dangerous situations can happen to anyone; however, for the Alpha Female, it is more intense as they are not used to being in vulnerable positions and they don't seek help right away. She is not immune to being "hunted." She may even handle the situation herself, which could end up being harmful or fatal.

Some Alpha Males interviewed for this book chose to specifically date Alpha Females, or so they thought. Their stories conveyed that they felt once the women started dating them, they became less Alpha-like, which they claimed was a turn off. The larger questions posed to the men were: "Were these women true Alpha Females, as the real ones do not lose their Alpha-ness?" or "Given the common factor was the man in this case, those women were augmented Alpha Females and in noticing those men were insecure in themselves and certain areas, decided to feed their egos and tone down their Alpha qualities to appease them? This would mean that the men were not real Alpha Males to start." The looks on the men's faces to the fact that they were the catalyst to results they received were astounding and they had to question their reality if *they* were truly Alpha.

Regarding the next steps of engagement, marriage, and family, Alpha Females usually are not eager be tied down by marriage and children. This does not mean they do not want to be in a solid relationship; but, they do not believe it has to be defined by conventional social standards. Being single does not equate to being alone or lonely. The ones that decide to marry usually do later in life and may have one child, if any. They like children, but also understand the level of commitment and impact to their lives, which may not be a good tradeoff for them. If they decide to have a child, they may hire a nanny, for they are not the doting wife or over-nurturing "June Cleaver" mother. Many of them would rather have an eternal engagement that ensures a sense of freedom and individuality. In many cases what has been witness throughout time that these women make the choice more with their minds than their hearts. Many times the level of commitment from exclusivity to marriage has an underlying tie to a logical/business sense. This does not mean that she does not have feelings for her man; it does mean her decisions are not driven by her emotions.

Through all this, she expects her man to be on his "A" game and will support him to get it back when needed. Make no mistake, gentlemen: Either bring your "A" game or it's "game over."

CHAPTER FIVE

The Bedroom: Who's The *Real* "Master"?

*"In the case of very fascinating women,
sex is a challenge, not a defense."*
—Oscar Wilde

This insight by Oscar Wilde holds truer for none other than the Alpha Female. Throughout history women were shamed, branded, exiled, and destroyed for embracing, exercising, and exposing their libidos. They were taught their bodies were for procreation, out of duty and obligation, but they were never to enjoy sexual intimacy. Those that defied the "system" were branded as whores, harlots, and Jezebels. In contrast, men were expected to be experienced at an early age, engaged in as many sexual experiences as possible, and were rewarded for their conquests. After decades of sexual revolution and women's rights movement, the double standards still exist. Yet, throughout history, those women who defied the sexual status quo were usually those that men found most fascinating. Ironic. Alpha Females are definitely the ones to bring the challenge to the bedroom and beyond; they're discreet, as with most of their life. Most men are puzzled by an Alpha Female's sexuality. They are left wondering, "Who's the real master?" Exploring her boudoir, see if you can figure it out.

Sexual Control: Mind, Body & Soul

Corin, who was not in attendance at the past few happy hours, is also a friend of CJ. Corin's position keeps her on the move two-thirds of the year; airports and hotels are second homes to her.

She's the girl who is intelligent, popular, not loud and overstated, well-rounded, and has more guy friends than girlfriends. She had a couple close girlfriends as a part of her inner circle in high school and college; compared to them, she played the field. She always enjoyed dating a variety of men (not meaning that she was having sex with all of them), enjoyed their company and, from some, what they did for her sexually. Her friends knighted her "the playette" of the group. She never fancied herself as such; she just knows what she likes, understands her sensuality, and is not afraid to leverage it for her goal—for her libido to be fed.

As she matured, she focused on her career. Now, she travels for work and for pleasure. Domestically and abroad, Corin has a "friend" or two in every city. At this point in her life, she does not want to be tied down, so having great friends across the globe keeps her company, and satisfied.

One of her acquaintances, Bryce, is a fitness model whom she met at a fashion event. They have always been sexually flirtatious, but both acknowledge that Bryce knows he has the looks and body that turns women's heads. Bryce believes that he can have Corin at any time with the "hooked on him" result. He does not know, however, that Corin has mentally placed him in the "one and done" category; she's awaiting the right opportunity to complete her mission.

Corin travels to Bryce's town and informs him of her presence; she'll be there for both business and personal events. Bryce invites her over for a home-cooked dinner and cocktails at his place when she first arrives. As the night winds down, they sit on the couch to watch a sports game, enjoying cocktails, and talking about their lives. Corin excuses herself to restroom after a few cocktails flowed through her. When she returns, much to her surprise, Bryce is standing there completely in the buff, "ready" for action. Initially, Corin was slightly startled as this was completely unexpected from just sitting on the couch watching television; she quickly composes herself, looks him over, noting his almost flawless physique. Although this is an extremely enticing proposition for Corin, she approaches him fully clothed and whispers seductively in his ear how inappropriate it is for him to make such a presumption. She questions his perception of her. Bryce, feeling somewhat embarrassed and rejected, tries to convince her that he thinks the world of her implies that he believes she wants it as much as he does. She informs him that no one wants him more that he wants himself; she retrieves her keys and heads out the door. As she drives back to her hotel, Bryce texts and calls her to apologize for his behavior, saying he does respect her and he's really not "that type of guy." Corin, who believes that too, had to take a deep breath, play it cool, and take a cold shower.

During the next few days, Bryce asks for forgiveness. He invites her to a club where he and some of his friends are celebrating a birthday. Corin agrees, as she is now on the leisure part of her *trip. Bryce believes he can make her jealous by flirting with other women.*

Corin meets him and the group at a local hotspot. After having her luxury car VIP-handled, she walks into the club, looking stunning, and is greeted by Bryce and his friends. He says hello, then pulls another woman friend onto the dance floor. Corin, who does not seem to notice, makes her way to the upper deck to get a panther's view of the scene. She notices Bryce looking up at her, to ensure she sees him looking at her and to see if she is looking at him. Corin decides to turn up the heat and turns her attention to the strapping security men who have been watching her. She decides to give one of them her attention and they start to converse, as Bryce watches from below. One or two guys approach her to dance, which she does, but returns to her chosen security stud. They exchange numbers. She realizes it is now approaching 1:30 a.m. and she has an early workout. She whispers to her security friend that is was nice meeting him and makes her way downstairs to leave. Bryce is there to catch her, asking her to dance. She informs him about her early morning, but he convinces her for one quick dance. She cuts the dance short, buys him the drink of his choice, and heads for the door. He remarks, having had a few drinks, that he may see her a bit later. She laughs, informs him not to start something he cannot finish, gives him a hug and whispers her suite number in his ear.

Corin goes to her suite, takes a shower, and falls into bed. Later, she hears a knock at her door. It's 3:30 a.m. She opens the door to see Bryce standing before her. He walks in; she closes the door. Neither of them say a word. She stares at him, turns, and walks toward the bedroom. She stops him in the entry way, grabs a pillow and blanket, hands them to him and points to the chaise. He looks at her in disbelief. However, being tired and buzzed, he slinks over to the chaise, undresses, and lays down to fall asleep—wondering why she turned him down again. Angrily, he starts to doze off, when he feels someone watching him. His eyes focus on a silhouette of an open robe revealing a heavenly body sprinkled with silk and lace moving toward him. Before he can fully focus, the silhouette straddles him, licks him seductively up to his lips leading into a kiss, and whispers words too racy to mention, bringing him to instant extended arousal.

Before Bryce can tactically respond, she dominantly takes him into her, via multiple facets, which creates a euphoric state he had yet to experience. Bryce had not realized she strategically placed herself on top him to limit his range of access to her, therefore focusing him to enjoy the ride on her terms. Bryce's conflict between extreme sexual pleasure and the challenge of not being able to participate his way creates a competitive weakness that drives his senses to be heightened, giving him the unbridled sexual peak he tries to control. In her grasp, he cannot move as she whispers naughty challenges and ultimatums. Corin gets into his head in more ways than one. She adjusts to various positions, depths, and vibrations bringing Bryce back and forth to the edge of climax, keeping him in limbo until she decides to bring Round One to a close.

Bryce, always prideful on his manly physique and sexual prowess, now feels he has something to prove. Corin quenches her thirst with some champagne while letting Bryce get his mojo up for Round two through whenever she's done. She walks back to Bryce, looking at him with a sexy smirk. He decides to take a more assertive approach. As she turns to walk away, shaking her head that he was "all talk," he comes up behind her and pins her to the wall between the living area and bedroom, running his tongue from the dip in her back up to her neck. He turns her around to lift her up to taste what he recently experienced. He brings her to mount as he walks to the bed with her legs wrapped around him.

He takes more of a controlling position this round as he is determined to bring her to memorable ecstasy. "Now the fun begins," Corin thinks to herself, knowing Bryce's motivation and intent. She allows him to believe he is in control, figuring she'll make the most of it. Bryce is more intent on proving himself than he is focused on her, and believes he's pleasuring her due to the responses. As aesthetically pleasing as his nakedness is to the eye, he does nothing for her sexually. Corin thinks, "I could have had a V-8". Corin needs to take control of the situation. She slyly allows him to control the positions, but she uses her physical and psychological "devices" to control the sensitivity that takes men down climatic avenues and successfully shuts down Round Two. Bryce, unaware of who really had the power moves, tries to boast to Corin about his performance; but, her expression proves she's not impressed. He asks her about her level of satisfaction; her ho-hum answer floors him. He assures her he is the man he claims to be, requesting another round of activity. Corin manipulatively agrees hoping he'll step up his game and give her one of the best trysts of her life.

They enter a third, then fourth round of "fun" when Corin realizes Bryce's bedroom compatibility with her is little to non-existent. Again, she allows him to believe he has full control of the situation, waiting to experience all he has to offer. Although his performance improves, it does not compare to other lovers she's had. Granted, within the hotel and not at her "fun palace" within her home, she feels limited on what she can do to heighten his pleasure beyond previous measure. She finally asks him softly if some of the moves, touches, and caresses he executes work for other women and, if so, that she's not other women. Bryce never realizes with the transition of control takes place, but before he knows it, instead of him having her feeling weak from multiple orgasms, he starts feeling the intense pleasure from what he experienced the first round. He wants to fight the weakness of giving into her, but he cannot, knowing he has fallen prey to her sexual spell once again. The art of manipulative control gives Corin more of the climatic pleasure than Bryce provides. She has him under her spell, can get him to do anything, allow her to do anything to him as she pushes his limits to the point of pleading. She ensures she closes the final round by bringing him to another climatic high; hands him his clothes, has his shoes at the door, and tells him to drive home safely as she kisses him politely on the cheek. Bryce is stunned and has no time to react. So, he leaves. Corin shakes her head, jumps into the shower laughing, and takes a quick nap to make her early morning workout.

The next day Bryce texts and calls Corin about their time together; asking when they can get together again. She informs him

93

it was a one-time deal, to never be recaptured, but they can always be friends. Confused, he believes he can convince her otherwise. He's never allowed to do so, thus creating a slight sexual tension between them with the experience forever etched in his memory.

Alpha Females epitomize the Dr. Jekyll/Ms. Hyde personality when it comes to their bedroom antics. These ladies leverage their seductive charisma in business and pleasure. The difference lies in the "always professional/business-minded" persona which demands the upmost respect, to the "behind closed doors/highly sexual" reality of her personal life. They usually keep the two lives completely separate, never linking. They are not nymphomaniacs (although some would like to label them as such); their high libidos, congested schedules, and immunity to "getting emotional" enables them to quench their sexual desires without attachment, like most men. More than the physical act itself, the ability to exert control (at times, power) creates the orgasmic euphoria for them.

Alpha Females continually calculate how to reach their goals or attain the conquests they seek. There are some basic labels they use to classify the "target" when they see it: "One and done," "one-night stand," "potential relationship," "dip-back worthy," and "the challenge," to name a few. Do not confuse the "one and done" with the "one-night stand," as they are different. A "one-night stand" is a "one and done," but the "one and done" is not always a "one-night stand."

For the first two categories, men need to realize there is no second chance to make a first impression. She attends happy hours, works out in the gym, or stops by the local coffee shop/mall where she may identify what she wants. For the one-night stand, she may opt to leave their names a mystery, as not to feel obligated to acknowledge him again.

In Corin's story, the Alpha Female utilized the male ego to draw him in, always having the power in the situation, and pretends to give him control, only to manipulate the ultimate power move in the end. He did not get the euphoric cuddling afterward, which he likely expected her to want. (Cuddling is rare with Alpha Females. They are quick to disclose "It's hot! Need some space to cool off," and go from orgasm to executing the next thing on their schedule, via laptop, cell, or physical fitness activity.) The internal etching of the pleasure, coupled with a male's dented ego, forever keeps a small spark of hope to have another love-making event. Alpha Females know they will always have a button to push or internal lever to pull.

Alpha Females keep their "game" tight at all times. Nothing turns them off in the bedroom more than a man not properly "groomed." Alpha Females require their men to be manscaped. The areas include facial, chest, back and nether regions to be trimmed to bare minimum or waxed completely. The rule stands as "Bush = No Brains." Those men who turn her off from first meeting, lack of conversation, or lack of proper grooming, are referred to as "no brainers."

The conflict of interest for the Alpha Female in the bedroom is the art of keeping, or fully relinquishing, control. There's rarely a time where her partner leaves satisfied beyond his expectations, as this is a part of her ego and competitive nature ensuring she has him weakened so she can sexually do with him as she pleases. She'll call things to an end before a poor performance. At the same time, there are times she yearns for the man to exert his overwhelming masculinity, be assertive, and take control to the point of pure ecstasy for her. Men, there is a difference with assertive, aggressive, dominance in a highly sensual manner versus just a rough-and-tumble juvenile manner; the latter ends the night immediately. Usually, Alpha Males are able to ascertain the difference in when she will allow herself to relinquish control and flash some vulnerability, not necessarily the power. Once an Alpha Female knows the man cannot match or exceed her endurance, fantasies, or fetishes, he becomes her "bitch in the bedroom," which kills her interest in him. She does not show all the layers to her sexuality to every partner; the guy has to be one she'll never see again or someone she trusts, showing discretion and respect with the openness to experiment to the point of, but not limited, to S&M.

Upon meeting a potential sexual partner, if the guy displays the "Chatty Patty" syndrome, she'll be turned off. He never becomes a further thought.

The Bedroom and Beyond: All Sex, Few Lies, No Video

CJ and Kaden, now engaged, discover they have more in common than they first imagined. During their first few times together, they discovered they were highly compatible sexually. Their sexual rendezvous were not only intimate but became more competitive as they both felt pride of who could "out do or outlast" the other in the endurance and pleasuring categories. They challenge each other's imagination from various positions, places, roles, and props. CJ enjoys when Kaden exerts his ability to "release" her of being in control; although she continues to maintain her power.

One evening, after they had become officially engaged, CJ and Kaden were on the couch, with CJ lying against him taking the time to watch one of their favorite shows. Television becomes rare as they both are continuously busy. They start to converse on their "hidden" fantasies that either they want to revisit or have yet to experience. They agree that their commitment to each other cannot be shaken. The next level of intimacy fantasies would only strengthen their bond.

Kaden tentatively describes a fantasy that includes CJ and another woman. He attempts to appear as if he broaches the subject of the threesome in a shy, yet seductive, manner to CJ; she saw through the façade. He gives a general description of the fantasy for the main focus is for him to have the threesome with two women. CJ

97

pretends to have to give the idea some consideration, as to not tip him off that she desires the same—but with Kaden and another man. She informs Kaden that she would be willing to fulfill his threesome desire, if he fulfills hers. She explains she wants Kaden and another man. Kaden is taken by surprise as he is not used to women making such a request. She informs him that they do not have to touch each other and that the experience focuses solely on her, just as she wants his experience to focus on him. He does not know that this would not be a first indulgence of this type of threesome for CJ; not a usual routine, but she had the initial experience years prior. Kaden goes quiet as he has to think about CJ's request, knowing that if he does not agree there is no way in hell he will get his request fulfilled. Kaden agrees. The couple discusses certain terms: they have to approve of the other person for both indulgences, the person must be a stranger to both of them, and CJ's request is to be fulfilled first. CJ knows the tentativeness of Kaden of her with him and another man, so to mitigate the risk of Kaden rescinding on his side of the agreement, he must oblige her first. Kaden agrees to the terms set by CJ. A ménage-a-trois venture will not be the end of their erotic journey; more of the beginning.

CJ already had a person in her sight whom she wanted to be the invited guest to the intimate party. The man was a person she had seen at the gym. She did her homework to find his hangouts to create the "stranger" encounter to Kaden. The man had flirted with CJ before when he ran into her at a high-end store, but nothing had gone further. CJ learned of a few of the hotspots he attends and, on the night of approach, ensures that she and Kaden would be in attendance.

The night arrives where CJ and Kaden go out for a night on the town to the spot where her unknowingly guest, Kaz, attends. They scope the scene; have a couple of drinks at the bar to scope out potential participants in their quest. As they are scoping the area, both CJ and Kaden lock eyes on Kaz. Kaz's stunning looks, chiseled physique, hypnotic voice, and overall great personality made him attractive to most women and buddies with most men. Kaz spots CJ at the bar and makes his way over near her to order a drink. CJ officially introduces herself to him as if she had never seen him before. Kaz looks past her at the bar and sees Kaden; Kaz senses a slight game being played, so he pretends to have never seen CJ, politely introduces himself to her, and then to Kaden. They converse over drinks, laughing and having fun. CJ, while flirting with Kaz, starts to inquire about his romantic life and desires. During the course of conversation, Kaz asks CJ to dance with him. She does. On the dance floor, he whispers to her about how he wants to be with her if only for one night. He discloses his desire since seeing her in the gym for the very first time. CJ smiles inside as she delivers the offer for Kaz to gain his wish in addition to partaking in an intense sexual experience.

Kaz initially gives CJ the "Are you serious?" look to the direction of the conversation. CJ communicates this would be the only way he could have her and guarantees he never has to touch Kaden—the focus would be on her. She explains the rules of no evidence, no regrets, no judgments, no inhibitions, and no disclosure of the unleashed pleasure of the night. Kaz, curious as to what the night has in store, agrees to the terms that he believes will fulfill his desire.

They return to the bar noticing Kaden chatting it up with a young woman showing high interest in him. Kaden dismisses the woman upon CJ's return. CJ gives Kaden the silent signal of Kaz's agreement. They have a couple of additional drinks at the bar, and dance a bit more before leaving for the afterhours of fun.

They return to CJ's place, have a drink or two, and quickly enter the lair of pleasure where she is the center of attention. CJ's seductive movements have the men competing for her attention. They pleasure every inch of her body, with every part of theirs, while CJ maintains her power by exerting and releasing sexual control throughout the night. At one point, she restrains both men to allow her to experimentally bring them to various heights of pleasure that they would never request. Pleasuring them in ways that bring out their hidden desires boosts her ego. The final round comes to a climax with CJ in the middle, facing Kaden, with Kaz behind her. As they come to their climatic peaks, CJ and Kaden share an intense kiss, while Kaz whispers in her ear how he is and has been in love with her. CJ dismisses the declaration as nothing more than a climactic reflex. The guys fall into a slumber, but CJ retires to her steam shower, emerges immaculately clean, and wakes Kaz to politely show him the way out. Kaz respectfully abides, mentioning he is aware she heard his declaration and it had nothing to do with the heat of the moment. CJ coyly smirks and gives him a peck on the cheek and closes the door. She walks to her den where she takes a nap on her favorite chaise only to get back to normal business within a few hours.

The next day, CJ returns to her normal life as if the night never existed; quietly reveling in the "red carpet" service she experienced. She and Kaden return to their high-traffic schedules. He's traveling for the next two weeks. Thoughts of "the night" replay in his mind where he realizes it brought about another level within CJ he had not quite experienced; or, at least he believed. He was used to being the more sexually adventurous one in relationships; he wondered if he'd finally met his match. Kaden became accustomed to having his trysts while on the road, could charm his way out of a tight spot if caught by his current girlfriend, and would be confident of her monogamy no matter the situation. He understood this relationship was very different as CJ has all the same options he has and more. He knows if he expects to explicitly broach monogamy assurance with CJ, he cannot make one false move of breaching the pact. He knows he loves CJ and she is the one for him, but it does not stop him from wanting the occasional tryst to keep things interesting.

They both have high-powered, intense career positions. Most people in these positions find other outlets for release. Kaden, returning from his business trips, approaches CJ about an "elite" club they should check out. CJ's disinterest perplexes Kaden given their sexual intimacy pushes the limits of fun to untapped desires; what's behind closed doors stays there. She informs him of the need to always be discrete as not to affect their professional lives. Actually, she was "over it" as she had lived abroad and had the mindset of "been there, done that." CJ, much like Kaden, cares for him deeply, but it does not stop her from wanting the occasional tryst.

CJ assures Kaden the "elite" club scene experience could take place at home. CJ has more than one place of residence. Kaden had been to one of them, but was unaware of the other two. Kaden has no idea of what she meant by the comment, but allows the conversation to end. A few weeks later CJ and Kaden take a weekend trip to a place where she has a lavish, state-of-the-art condo. Kaden, already surprised, has no idea just how surprised he will be. As they lay by the fire, Kaden makes his advances toward CJ. She backs away and walks slowly down the stairs. Kaden follows her to a nice room that he soon discovers has a hidden "fun room." She invites Kaden into the room with many capabilities to experience and experiment with various sexual eroticisms. She discloses to Kaden that only a select few know about the hidden room and he must sign a confidentiality agreement and waiver before entering or becoming a willing participant. Kaden chuckles, given he is her fiancé, then realizes she is serious about being confidential. He questions her trust of him as her fiancé. CJ explains she protects herself from legal issues and her right to privacy as this room is accessed on select occasions. She explains it is not a matter of trust; she protects her professional brand and financial estate. She poses the question to him: "Would you not do the same or something similar?" Kaden pauses in thought knowing he would protect himself in such a manner. He agrees to her terms and conditions, saying to her "This is why I love you; you never cease to amaze me." CJ's regality with the stealthy erotic edge, complimented by her panther-like strategic maneuvering and extreme intellect, draws Kaden's heart to her more than ever. The night between them lends itself pushing the limits of intimacy, trust, and control. Kaden always prides himself on his various techniques and endurance for lovemaking. CJ, aware of his ego, has an agenda to give Kaden an experience where fantasy blends reality, forever etching his memory. She brings him to a submissive-type arena of constraints, sensory stimulation/depravation, painful pleasure, and deep erotica that cannot be spoken.

Upon concluding the night's events, CJ asks an exhausted Kaden to leave the room for her to clean and sanitize. As he walks toward the door a small glimmer catches his eye. It is an emblem on a bracelet in the corner of a shelf; it looks familiar. As he walks out of the room, he remembers Kaz wearing an exact replica the night he met him—or, was it a replica? They spend the rest of the weekend resting and sipping wine. The image of the bracelet stays on Kaden's mind.

As they leave the hide-a-way and head back to their normal lives, CJ notices Kaden is rather quiet, but she says nothing. Once they arrive at Kaden's place he tells CJ he has early meetings and shall turn in early. She, seemingly indifferent, leaves for her place. Kaden stews over whether or not to bring up the bracelet he saw in the room and if it belonged to Kaz. It keeps him up at night as he wonders if it does how long it has been there; was it before he and CJ started dating? Was it after he met Kaz at the club with CJ?

Thoughts of Kaz with CJ in the "fun room" kept him agitated all night.

During the week, CJ travels for business and returns home on Friday to see Kaden waiting for her at door. She invites him in, informing him of her exhaustion from her travel. He ignores her remark quickly bringing up the bracelet, which starts an interrogation. CJ looks at him with the expression of "Really?" She informs him she is not in the mood for his accusations and interrogation attempts, requesting he leave. Kaden is livid demanding straight answers. CJ calmly requests he reconsiders his position carefully before opening doors he's not ready to walk through. Kaden's emotional state overrides his common sense and dismisses her warning. He claims if she does not provide straight answers, their relationship is over. CJ, pouring herself a light glass of wine, agrees to converse about what Kaden has on his mind. He inquires about the bracelet, disclosing he remembers Kaz wearing one just like it the night he "joined" them. He immediately starts in on if it belongs to Kaz, the "whens," "how longs," etc. CJ calmly sips her wine, waiting for him to pause. She responds to him the bracelet belonged to Kaz; he knew she admired it and insisted she keep it. He inquires why it was in the "hidden room." She responds, "That is where he insisted I keep it." Kaden becomes stunned. He asks if she had known Kaz before the "initial meeting." She looks at Kaden with a condescending judgmental look of her own. He accuses her of being unfaithful and lying to him. She admits the night in the club was not her first time meeting him, but nothing had happened between them. Before Kaden could start to chastise her, she quickly stops him saying, "Why are you surprised, I said nothing to you about the tryst you had while on your business trip to Miami?" CJ goes into detail about the woman he was with, delivering a jaw-dropping bomb on Kaden. Before he can start to deny, she informs to him there is no reason for him to ask how she knows—no she did not follow him or have him followed, just for him to understand she knew when it happened, which was soon after they were engaged. She explains to him that since he was the one who proposed and insisted they be mutually exclusive, which CJ agreed, he breached the commitment and put the relationship in a different state. Kaden is not sure what to say at this point as now he realizes CJ orchestrated the "meeting" of Kaz and the events to follow. Knowing he's busted about the tryst he had in Miami paints him into a corner of not being able to blame CJ for the initial breach of trust. She tells him to evaluate what kind of a relationship he wants; she cares for him, but as he can plainly see, he opened the door for the relationship to become "all sex, some lies, and no video," which is her right to exercise. She tells him he cannot require something from her that he cannot adhere to himself. She escorts him out of her house. (Yes, she left the bracelet there on purpose for Kaden to "discover.")

He sits in his car for a moment, trying to reconcile his bruised ego, his genuine feelings for CJ, yet realizing his infidelity has created hypocrisy. During the drive home, he knows he has a decision to make: to find a way to convince CJ to be mutually exclusive and that she can trust him to commit to the same, or rethink the relationship and if he can handle dating "himself."

Alpha Females are always about their "Dr. Jekyll/Ms. Hyde" power persona in their professional and personal lives. The power manifests itself differently in each. Although they are usually those to never quite fully commit through conventional means of marriage, they do enjoy meaningful, intimate relationships. They can be monogamous, although doing so is a challenge.

The Alpha Female prides herself on being the standard of excellence in the bedroom, much as she is in the boardroom. She compares to her Alpha Male counterpart when being the center of sexual attention, creating sexual challenges, and pushing the sexual limits of herself and her partner. Don't make the mistake of considering her to be a freak or whore for that would bring about undo consequences. She is neither. She embraces her sexual desires, her power and confidence to exercise them, and her need for variety. No other parts of their lives are conventional; why would their sex lives? Not all Alpha Females have a "fun room;" their sexual fun varies from Alpha to Alpha. However, even those that exhibit the minimal levels of sexual openness often compare much higher to the average female. If approached about a threesome, do not be surprised if she insists she is in the center of two men. It is, in fact, all about her.

The Alpha Female competes in high-performing, high-pressure positions within heavily male-dominated industries. Much like her male counterparts, there are times she wants her partner to assert control in the bedroom; to allow her to decompress, to let go *almost* to submission. However, when there are stressors or power imbalance, her "dark side" can appear. At that point, her sexual power can push the limits to their brink. She'll exert power to out-perform her sexual partner in every possible way. She'll create such a euphoric state that the sex partner does not realize the limits he allows or embraces. She creates the illusion it is all about him, that she is there only to pleasure him; but, the illusion is anything but true. These can range anywhere from painful pleasure to multiple sensory deprivation to erotic affixation and more.

When these ladies commit to monogamy, it is a level of delicate trust that hinges on the authenticity of their partner's commitment. Their radar is always scanning for breach of negotiated terms and conditions. They do not wear their hearts on their sleeves, so they may not react immediately to discovering infidelity. Yet, a strategic plan is always in motion to gain the upper hand, express wrath, and win in the end.

She returns easily to Jekyll: with no trace, no evidence, nor hint of her erotic life. Even the participant of these events questions if the memory was real, which screws with his psyche, creating heightened attraction.

CHAPTER SIX

The Conventional Contradiction

There is nothing conventional about the Alpha Female, with one exception: She contradicts the perceived societal norms. Movies, music, television, history, and society in general depict women as objects needing and wanting to be saved by someone, or something, larger than them. The Alpha Female defies this depiction, this perception, which society perpetuates. Society views her decisions, actions, and beliefs as not only unconventional for a woman, but condemns the perceived abnormality and tries to "cure the defect" or destroy what it cannot cure. The Alpha Female embraces her normality, drawing admiration and disapproval from the masses. Her "abnormal" beliefs span from religion to relationships, family, friends and foes, spirituality to sexuality, and all areas between. Peek into the lives of a few Alpha Females' to gain insight to their "normality."

Saint with a Past or Sinner with a Future?

Chasity is a young lady belonging to a very religious family. Her father was a highly respected leader of the church and mother was thought to have the highest of virtues among the members. She and her siblings were strictly reared according their religion, taught the customary roles of men and women, and at the center of their lives stood the church and its religious beliefs. Chasity, forced to follow the rules, never believed in the views of the church, even as a little girl. From birth, she stood out as the "black sheep" of the family and congregation by competing with the boys, speaking her mind, challenging the religious teachings, and behaving unladylike. Her father continually disciplined her "defiance," using corporal punishment and stripping every conceivable privilege from her to the point of being extremely abusive, in all aspects. Although the other siblings may not have fully enjoyed the upbringing, they dared not to defy the master of the home and family, their father. The more Chasity's father worked to reprogram and control her, the more she held steady and clashed with him. Reaching a crossroad, she began compartmentalizing the situation, becoming the chameleon who appeared to conform to the rest of the family and the congregation—and surviving the abuse.

Maturing into adulthood, he continues to interject religious teachings on sexuality, marriage, the role of women in the home and world, children, divorce, and "fire and brimstone" rules into her life. Although she compartmentalizes her internal beliefs for the sake of survival, they continue to exist within her. Entering college slightly later than most, she gains the respect of her friends who viewed her as the "mom" figure. The young ladies reach out to her for advice, guidance, and approval. College kids are known for being wild and risky. Chasity reminds the free-wielding young ladies of the spiritual views of life, the expectations of relationships, sex, risky behavior, and the temptations other seedy vices would have on their souls and salvation. While she gives the virtuous reminders, most do not realize she struggles internally with her "programming" and her true beliefs and desires.

Following the common progression of graduating from college, getting married, and becoming a mother, she continues to struggle with the core beliefs she worked hard to keep hidden. The internal struggle leads to multiple bouts of depression, to the point of suicidal contemplations. Her inner wiring programs her away from aligning to the typical God-approved submissive woman of whom the church preaches; divergent from the passive, non-assured woman that her father praises and weaves into the family thread as the definition of a "good" woman.

From the outside looking in, Chasity's life appears to be picture perfect. She has a college degree, a successful husband, a beautiful home, a beautiful child, and everything the American dream has to offer. Her husband notices a few questionable behaviors, but dismisses them as hormonal. The perfect external and internal storms brew until the day that she chooses to live her beliefs and truths or perish in the perceived perfection. She named the day "Alpha Day," or "AD."

Before "AD," Chasity lived the "real" her behind closed doors. She started a side business under an alias, kept business meetings, social meetings, and travel secret from her family and most of her friends. She unleashed her seductive savvy as she had been sexually repressed as well. Given she had not gained much experience in her twenties, she chose and collected lovers like a high-caliber classic car collector and stored them on a shelf until she wanted to take one for a good ride. What appeared to be the "dark side" of life for Chasity *actually was the light of truth; while the perfect-life perception represented the real dark side.*

On Alpha Day, Chasity confesses to her husband her unhappiness with her life and their marriage, and her multiple infidelities. She informed him that she would no longer pretend to lessen herself and to preach to others what she did not believe herself. She confesses to him that among the multiple adulterous relationships, she had become pregnant twice; she was not sure of their paternity and did not want to have additional children, so she terminated the pregnancies. Although she cared for her husband, marriage was not important to her and she did not want to be married. Topping it all off, she discloses that he was never able to satisfy her sexually, which launched her to look elsewhere. The news devastates her husband, upsets the family balance, and creates the ultimate controversy to the conventional normal. She timed the confession such that it happened on a Friday. Chasity surprised her husband with a morning sexual experience that would be forever etched in his memory. After the morning fun, she breaks the news to him and, by noon, a court processor arrives at their home to serve him with divorce papers. In less than 24 hours she had moved herself and child to a brand new home and purchased a new luxury vehicle to start life anew as if her previous life never existed.

Chasity's pendulum swung from the appearance of Bible-thumping, status quo, chaste female to the strategic, assertive, business savvy, multiple-lover female she previously would have referred to as whorish. The equilibrium imbalance usually takes place earlier on for an Alpha Female as they seek answers to their

112

makeup, despite the societal teachings, and harness the inner power they possess. Chasity experiences the imbalance in her later years, creating a major inner struggle for her that manifests itself in areas of hoarding, extreme emotionally detached promiscuity, heightened sexual deviance, and complete detachment of emotions from others, all in the name of restoring control and the equilibrium to her life. The more control she exerts, the more she risks to lose, including her health, her child, her heart, and her stability. On the outside, Chasity appears to others as a rock that has it all under control. Her friends and former college mates are shocked to see her in this light. She continues to command attention in social settings, create the business connections, provide the best for her child, and present herself as a class act to all those she meets. Behind closed doors, she knows that she has to fully regain the power she relinquished years ago. She accepts that the church, family, and society look upon her as the "cold bitch" that cheated and left her husband, desecrating family values. She seeks therapy to make peace with the conflicting beliefs—those wired within her and those that were abusively thrust upon her. Although deep down inside, she really does not care about what others think about her; it is her own high expectations of self that she has to reconcile, and embrace her societal contradictive DNA. Can she ever regain full equilibrium? Does she?

This snippet of Chasity's life depicts a rarer case for Alpha Females, but one that exists. Recalling earlier discussions, true Alpha Females are born immune to reprogramming attempts and become chameleons to navigate situations, but their Alpha traits are never fully hidden. They push back or simply disregard their parents, religion, and family members that attempt to make them something other than who they are, even when abused.

Chasity's story exposes an exception: when a true Alpha Female suppresses her beliefs, behaviors, choices, intelligence, and libido due to heavy abuse starting early in life. It becomes merely a temporary survival tactic. Her ability to compartmentalize and survive becomes a double-edged sword as the perceived repression creates an internal struggle of appearing to conform to the dictation of societal norms of religion, sex, marriage, roles, and so forth, while her true beliefs contradict those accepted societal norms. What makes her different from other women with the same upbringing? Most women would adapt to the situation and be swayed to believe as they were taught. They would submit themselves to the abuse, never finding them outside of it mentally or emotionally. They struggle to compartmentalize their libido from emotions, religion from spiritual, control from power. For most women, the abuse would bring them to the brink of self-destruction; with the Alpha Female, her own internal belief battle risks her perseverance. Most women "do" because they have to; Alpha Females "do" because they know they have the power to "choose to."

People whore themselves for status, money, sex, power, career, and much more, yet not labeled as such. Given the irony of Chasity becoming unchaste, should she wear the scarlet letter of a whore? If yes, then why? Would a man be branded in the same fashion for being assertive, career-focused, dating more than one woman, sex with more than one woman? Is it a double standard that society has not accepted: Is the Alpha Female, who is the Alpha Male in female form, the contradiction?

Marriage & Children: Why Have Either?

Cydney, a young woman on the rise in every aspect of her life, plans a long weekend trip with the girls for her thirtieth birthday. She invites Peyton and Campbell, ladies she has known for quite some time, extending the invitation to her inner, trusted circle. Three successful, professional women look forward to having fun in the sun, relaxing over cocktails, and enjoying the celebration of her birthday. Peyton is a year younger than Cydney, while Campbell is a few years older than both of them.

While on the trip, Cydney receives a "Happy Birthday" call from her mother, only to hear her mother express concern of her being single and childless. (This topic comes forth multiple times from family, friends, co-workers, and other people she meets, creating an intrusion, a disturbance of judgments with the poking of pressure to adhere to societal expectations.) After the call, she quickly grabs a stiff drink and joins the other two ladies lounging on the beach. She shares the conversation which sparks an elaborate debate and discussion among the women. Cydney does not see the big deal about being married or having kids, as neither was ever in her vision for her life. She thinks, "If marriage and kids are not important to her, why are they important to everyone else around her for her?" She enjoys dating and admits she is willing to commit up to an engagement.

Peyton looks at Cydney with confusion and asks why she has no interest in marriage and children. Peyton discloses she dreams of her wedding day, wedding dress, husband, and children. "What woman doesn't want a husband and children? A wedding? To live the American dream of the perfect family?" she asks Cydney. Meanwhile, Campbell sits back, sips on her drink, listening to the conversation. Cydney discloses to the ladies she never fanaticized of a wedding, husband, or children while growing up. She loves men and pictures herself, at most, engaged to a successful and powerful man who completes her perfect power couple. She brings up the religious and societal pressures to be monogamous and settle down, therefore solidifying the perception of the sanctity of marriage. She communicates the snarky comments of being called "selfish" when much older women hear that she has no desire to have children, as they believe all women should have at least one child. She also gets the question, "Why not, aren't you attracted to men?" which steams her up and creates laughter within her at the same time (given she views as other people's ignorance/stupidity) they don't know that she keeps a few great guys on the dating roster at all times.

Cydney knows Peyton puts pressure on her beau to propose so that she marries by age 30. Cydney remarks she believes that people who want to be married should be, but neither society, religion, nor law has the right to dictate how she commits to a relationship. She says she never wanted the title of "wife," taking vows in a church does not guarantee monogamy or commitment from either party, she already has a last name, and does not need the validation of a "princess day." She does not want a "husband" title for the man she commits to either. She is willing to be a fiancé, but does not want to be married. She poses the question, "After engagement, what is the value add of being married?" She admits that she is not a "June Cleaver" nurturer (and never desires to be seen as such), she's focused on her career and personal goals, adores children as long as they are not hers and has no desire for diaper changes and the impact a child would have on her life. She does not want to be tied down and loves her power of freedom. She continues to say that these beliefs do not make her less of a woman and she does not care what people think about her decisions; but, she expects respect from them. Peyton says that Cydney could be perceived as being "feminist" and that others have asked her about Cydney's sexual preference because Cydney keeps her personal life so private. She informs Cydney that her views may give others the wrong impression. Cydney, staring at Peyton like a panther assessing its prey, informs Peyton that the mere fact that people will always judge is the main reason she shares her personal life only with a select few. She tells Peyton that one's view of marriage and kids does not define their sexuality, and that she is not "dick-matized" by every man she meets or who feeds her ego with empty compliments of what they believe she wants to hear, like most women do. She shakes her head at Peyton with pity for being a regular chic, informing her that if Peyton chooses to live her life on the basis of others, Peyton is more than free to do so; but, she doesn't and does not need nor seek their approval. Peyton freezes from Cydney's cold stare, feeling as though she is peering directly into her soul.

Campbell, listening and grinning while their views and beliefs are shared, chimes in on the subject. She tells them she was married briefly during her mid-twenties. She understands Cydney's position, but buckled under the pressure of what society says success looks like for a woman. She explains to both of them that no "one right" decision exists and while most women do dream of wedding days, wedding dresses, and so forth, there are certain women who truly do not want the ceremony, the wife title, or the typical "normal" family. They can be in a committed relationship, but will not be confined to labels and typical, female-defined roles. She lends the advice of not succumbing to the pressures placed by society and family, rushing into a decision that she may not want. She encourages them to discover and acknowledge the type of man that compliments them. She explains to Peyton that the type of men that compliment women like them are highly intelligent, secure, in-demand, not afraid of losing a bet to them, confident but not arrogant, not led by ego, successful, go-getters, have high libidos, and challenge their intellect, body, and soul. A Beta Male, unless very, very secure within, does not pair well as his "Humpty Dumpty" ego (egg-shell fragility), toned-down drive, and need for nurturing will not understand nor appreciate them for their qualities. Rather, they begrudge them later. Campbell describes her ex-husband as a Beta Male who tried to disguise himself as an Alpha. She sensed the latter, but felt pressured to "have it all." In the few years they were married, he expected to be nurtured, did not understand nor want her next level of lifestyle, could not keep up with her drive or need for continual intellectual stimulation, and resented her full schedule. It ended somewhat peacefully after three years. Campbell admits that lessons were learned and she paid a hefty price.

Peyton looks stunned by the conversation. She asks several questions about why they believe as they do, implying they are abnormal due to an event in their lives. By this time in the conversation, the drinks have evolved from light and frilly to those with "liquid courage," allowing the ladies to share deeper insights, beliefs, and experiences. Peyton asks the ladies if they are afraid of dying alone, and why not have the "knight in shining armor" to take care of them, and don't they want the unconditional love that only a child can give? In response, Campbell offers insight into how she and Cydney are wired. They are not afraid of dying alone; and, the fact that they may be alone does not make them lonely. They can be in a committed relationship; they just do not want to be classified or perceived as "weaker" women. They are very attracted to men, but do not look for one to take care of them, as they can support themselves. As for needing the unconditional emotion, Campbell tells her that they are emotionally self-sufficient; they have emotions, but are not emotional. As for relationships, before committing to one, which may or may not happen, they date several men who must be able to keep up intellectually and sexually to barely maintain their interest.

The ladies communicate they are spiritual, but may not agree or conform to organized religion beliefs, especially when it comes to prescribed gender roles, women body choices, marriage, and so forth. Peyton absorbs the conversation, but continues to internally question the "Why?" believing these ladies are defective or somehow misguided. The ladies continue to enjoy their weekend, celebrating Cydney's birthday.

The classic fairytale told to women, from the time they are able to watch princess movies and read bedtime stories, is that they are to meet a charming prince, marry shortly after, birth 2.5 kids, buy a home with the white picket fence, and live happily ever after. This classic fairytale does not exist much with the Alpha Female. Although they want relationships, they do not feel that they need them. For the most part, Alpha Females do not need to be tied down in marriage or have children. If they decide to have offspring, rarely does it exceed one. Most are questioned by other women (and some men) on their sexuality because they are not married by a certain age or have chosen not to have children. The fact that they choose not to officially marry or have children does not mean that they don't like children or that that they are of a certain sexual preference. These areas of life can limit them and require emotional maintenance, which is not the focus of their time.

Some Alpha Females marry, but they may wait to do it later in life once their goals have been reached. Others prefer engagement as the limit of "official commitment." They simply try to remain drama-free. Relationship drama turns them off as they have extremely busy schedules, do not care for the emotional antics, and prefer to focus their time on the intense challenges they have set for themselves. Although they do love hard, their relationships are more focused on great business partnerships rather than romantic love and emotions. They want their men to be complimentary, not supplementary.

The Queenpin

Campbell's weekly schedule stays booked. It incorporates her job, gym, church, a few board memberships, friends, family and social organizations. Time being a precious resource, she focuses on ensuring she obtains the best deals, executes errands efficiently, and always receives red-carpet service. She finds time to provide listening and guidance for her family and close friends.

*Whether in social settings or personal life, she holds one standard: **Excellence**. A week in her life may go as follows:*

Having her car serviced, the men at the dealership know her vehicle by name, ensure the best techs perform maintenance and, once cleaned, store it inside the facility until she picks it up. She seductively rewards the loyal service by providing catered lunches to the team, relating kudos of the service to the local and corporate leadership (yes, she has network connections with corporate), and discussing the company's latest news and products with them. The guys know her expectations and the consequences to providing anything less than excellent service.

While traveling, she connects with the lead concierge at a top-rated hotel who ensures, anytime she stays, her suite includes complimentary champagne and appetizers; she greets the airline crew and socializes so they know her, and the car service/rental crews get a text before her arrival to have the vehicle of her choice in wait, as not to delay her schedule.

She takes her fitness and gym time seriously, as she incorporates five to six workouts a week within her busy schedule. She strategically knows the gym management, regional management, trainers, and key members—with keen awareness of the good-looking guys, their status, and whether they look to pursue/engage with her. Her social savvy opens doors of invites to elite events, complimentary treatments at the gym spa, and leverage for solicitation of her own company.

She selectively lends her time and name to participate on certain boards of directors and social organizational boards. Campbell's ability to power network enables her passions to create connections, leverage the abilities and networks of others creating the ultimate integrated networked web. Her noted lines "What do you need?... I'm connected with someone who... or, I have a friend who..." manages the perception as the go-to person that believes in the current purpose and can influence others to believe or lend a hand. She creates pivotal positions for herself; being the pivotal "node" between networks solidifies a person as the "go-to to get-through" czar, thus solidifying the role of Queenpin.

Her non-Alpha friends scratch their heads thinking "How does she do it?" "She's high-maintenance and demands special treatment." "Has she ever met a stranger?" "Who doesn't she know?" "How does she know...?" and so on. They underestimate the value of platinum social capital. Power networking encompasses a strategic mindset, genuine servitude, and the ability to create the right combination of connections, to mitigate a challenge or enhance opportunities expeditiously. Campbell naturally possesses these talents. She conducts herself with purpose and her attire signals anyone in her presence the expectation of performance excellence; this is a highly seductive recipe.

Her week is far from over as it incorporates her family and inner circle of friends.

Throughout her life, her family seeks her for consultation, guidance on various life situations ranging from major purchases to relationships. She has always assumed the responsibility of ensuring the social safety of her immediate family and if any outside influences attempt to take advantage, she immediately mitigates and/or eliminates the threat. The protective nature symbolizes the "L-word" (love), which she does not verbally express, but rather shows.

Campbell has emotions, but is not emotional. The absence of an emotional state creates the perception of "cold" or uncaring by her family and friends. With her busy schedule, she gets straight to the point, does not mind healthy conversation, but does not have time *for drama or discussions with no direction or decision. Her family and friends label her being "in business mode" at all times. Her heart exists, but is not worn on her sleeve as she rarely utilizes the "L-word". She respects her family, but does not seek their approval. Her love for those she truly cares about expresses itself through acts of protection, survival, encouragement, and being invited into her private life. She makes time for her family, taking calls from her mom and/or siblings and visiting between travel and work, but keeps a pace that oftentimes requires a call or text saying: "Where are you now?" Her family knows she cares; they also know she will not entertain any type of bullshit.*

When it comes to friends, her ability to create connections creates numerous relationships. However, she keeps her inner circle of true and trusted friends extremely small. She creates highly selective criteria for those she invites into her private life. Those who accept membership into her private circle sign up for very high expectations of platonic intimacy, honor, integrity, loyalty, and trust. She cares for these people, as she would her family, barring the bullshit.

She understands the selection, especially of non-Alpha Females, must be handled carefully. Non-Alpha Females usually follow conventional societal normality and beliefs and tend to be more emotional. They tend to have less than high-bar expectations for privacy and no drama; which differs with the unspoken rules of Alpha Females.

Campbell's inner circle seeks her advice, as they know they get the honest, no bullshit truth. Most times, Campbell simply asks questions that already have the answers, and realizes that she can be perceived as judgmental for it. Her attitude is, "If they did not want the feedback, they would not ask." Straight talk can stress friendships, especially when it comes to affairs of the heart. She recalls a time when she attempted to forewarn a long-time friend, Bryn, that she was being taken advantage of by a guy. She took the risk of bringing the actions to Bryn's attention, after asking her if she wanted to know. Bryn said "yes." Yet, Bryn was not receptive of the news and it stressed their friendship. The tipping point comes from the perception of where Bryn's loyalty lies: with believing Campbell, or taking, protecting and nurturing the side of the man wronging her.

If someone in Campbell's circle chooses to be loyal to an outsider or take their word over the years of long-term friendship, they will usually be exiled from the inner circle of trusted allies, never regaining that status. She applies a different set of expectations to assess her circle, including how communication and interactions are managed.

Campbell protects her inner circle many times without them being aware. She recalls another occasion where someone outside the circle, Beaux, tried to perpetuate a false accusation of someone in her circle of trust. He had no proof and claimed to be serving her friend's best interest; but, Campbell quickly recognizing the malicious motives of Beaux, used her charisma to draw out the motive, and orchestrated subtle movements from charm to seductive intimidation (lowering the pitch of her voice, signaling with her eyes, and eliminating the personal buffer zone), while calmly expressing that he ceases in his actions or would have to deal with her. Her over calm, exotic, feline movements created unease; yet, Beaux understood the promise of the consequence. She shut down the situation as the Queenpin, protecting the person in her circle without them ever knowing.

The Queenpin makes time for her inner circle and priorities the rest as her schedule allows. Although she enjoys being social, especially with close friends, solitude nourishes her mind and spirit, and rounds out her typical week.

The words of Fran Lebowitz, "Polite conversation is rarely either," questions the motive; as does the perception of the usual, routine, social interactions of an Alpha Female, which are rarely usual or routine. Her skill of creating the casual perception can easily be mistaken, especially from the opposite sex, as being lax or less aware. To those that make the misjudgment, the response can be socially or financially fatal. The Alpha Female, on the surface, socializes with the various people she meets throughout the course of her day. Mentally, she meets, greets, and files the people away in a mental database until they become a part of her network or stored until the need to pull their file again. These ladies quickly create virtual social cities, highways, and interstates with people, organizations, and businesses to the point they can modularly restructure the right combination for a purpose as if it were built of Legos®. The structures have the right people, with the right attributes, routed to the right networks. She expects loyalty from her close connections and she rewards for it. She always leaves an impression with those she connects, ranging from the tablespoon of honey to the teaspoon of vinegar. Her standard is **excellence**, not perfection, as she knows the difference. However, the excellence that she has within, and brings about in every aspect of her life, is often perceived as perfection.

An Alpha Female enjoys creating positive networks that are leveraged to help others. Her motivation to help others pairs with her own needs. The "honey" version of her seeks the opportunities for genuine servitude of the greater good. Many times the people she helps are unaware that she was the hidden catapult to their success; she keeps the information confidential. She prefers anonymity as not to overshadow the person's confidence, while enjoying the satisfaction of her flawless execution.

Her mob-boss style of protection seductively draws her circle closer. Her family knows the rules of interacting with them are simple: damn the dramatic, don't sugarcoat shit, and she'll annihilate their asses if they disrespect her. The same rules apply to her friends and intimate relationships. *She attempts to save all those she protects from themselves.*

Her internal rules, coupled with her protective nature, create a tug of war which, if not careful, can strain her emotionally and financially.

She tends to hang out with other Alphas, but will have a circle of non-Alphas (male and female) to add to the mix. She studies her circle of friends from a psychological level to lead them down a seductive path of her choosing. Her roles range from the logical lawyer to the smooth salesperson baiting them to do her bidding. She takes them out for dinner and drinks, invites them on nice vacations, and sets up spa events to intentionally expose them to the high-maintenance-yet-normal life of an Alpha Female. She knows the buttons to push and the levers to pull creating the seductive tension of mutual loyalty.

So, what about interaction with other Alpha Females?

The Queenpin Summit

Campbell and some of her other Alpha Female circle decide to meet for brunch and drinks at one of their favorite high-end bistros. The four of them are greeted by the owner and escorted in style to their own, private area which houses the best table.

They order libations and food while they discuss their schedules, compare notes on careers, relationships, and network strategies. The four Queenpins—Campbell, Cydney, Chloe, and Cara—create the presence of subtle décor equal to the likings of the "mob boss summit."

After brunch these ladies convene to a spa, where they continue their conversations. Although they have their own "family" circles, they all serve on a multiple corporate, social, and non-profit organization boards, with more than one of them residing as co-board members. As they relax in the steam room, a candid conversation starts on what is truly going on in each of their lives. Cydney, the youngest of the group, confesses to a situation where she had an intimate tryst with an executive within the company more than once; now, she has regrets and needs advice to navigate those waters. The ladies are silent for a second, then begin to ask questions to understand the lead up to the confessional. They give her advice on perceptions, discretion, and to maintain a good rule of being careful "not to shit where you eat because, in the end, you'll risk eating shit." They go around the room and share their experiences of either being approached or solicited in this manner and how they handled it.

Cara discloses that she is going to call off her engagement as she and her fiancé have been having issues. He has not been supportive of her fast-paced life, busy schedule, and career drive. He is driven and busy himself so, in theory, it should work; but, she feels he wants to compete with her more than be with her. She confesses that she believes that he is with her for status. She confesses that she had been living a lie in the perfection of her relationship and discloses the more in-depth details: Although they have great sex, she has known him to "step out" on her, yet he cannot handle when she has "steps out" on him. Not to mention the other areas where he works her nerves. She looks to the "Queenpin Summit" to gauge if she is over-reacting or if her instincts and decisions are valid. The ladies listen, ask a few pointed questions, and think for a moment. Campbell, who was previously married, offers some wisdom of not reacting too hastily, and to determine what things are acceptable, including "don't ask don't tell" trysts. All of the ladies agree that "great sex" could make a woman think twice—okay, three times— and chuckle it up. They ask if their high-powered careers and

*intense travel schedules can support monogamy, or is it a deal
breaker? Overall, they all weigh in on the situation, not the fiancé,
as to give honest points of view with support. They continue their
conversations sharing innermost thoughts and concerns.*

*The ladies leave the steam room and head to the pool for fun in
the sun and more libations. They know they look hot in their
swimwear and can turn the heads of men from various races and
cultures. They arrive on scene to their private cabana. As the first
round of drinks arrives, the ladies start to discuss the politics of the
boards they currently sit. As they take turns dipping in the pool, the
topic of agendas, leadership offices, and overall end-game results
that they seek start to surface. The ladies, almost with the psychic
ability to read each other's minds, strategically decide the fates of
board members, events, and platforms that will be supported,
sidelined and eliminated. They create the invisible remote of buttons
and levers to be used to influence the support, behaviors, and
motions of the right people, in the right places, at the right time. The
pact between them ensures that everyone has a role to play, executes
with excellence on cue, and that they have the psychological, non-
emotional game to pull it off. The finesse of it all is the fact that the
"chess" strategy would not be tied to them.*

*In the midst of additional drinks, pool dips, and looking sexy in
the sun, Chloe brings up an interesting topic that had been posed to
her, and that she noticed herself. "In the midst of navigating,
collecting information, being assertive, having a plan of action, and
being seductive, it seems that the levers and buttons of
manipulation are not executed between us instinctively as if there*

130

was an understood rule and honor code." The ladies, looking at each other with Queenpin grins, nod in agreement.

Alpha Females run in packs of maximum four at any given time. Sometimes, they hang out in pairs, or as a trio. Watching the Queenpin pack is like seeing music in motion: The score to the "Godfather" and the lyrics to "Wonder Woman" seem to herald them into any space they enter. Whether entering together or one-by-one, their presence is acknowledged, respected, and catered. From the scent of their perfume to the dip in their backs to when they stand, they are noticed.

The Queenpin looks to her equals for advice, support, and reality checks. She respects the same characteristics that she possesses. Psychologically, she understands the unwritten rules of being genuine with each other, otherwise they'll socially "sleep with the fishes."

The unwritten rules of Alpha Females among each other set them apart among women. The rules for their **circle** include: being genuine, creating no intentional psychological "seduction" attempts between them, being honest yet supportive when assessing another Alpha's problem, avoiding "mean girl" behaviors and simple bitch drama, and rejecting "Dime or Dick" chic behavior (D.o.D women are those who sell out their friends/family for a dime or a dick). The unwritten rules regarding their **relationships** are: listen, but never insult her man when she may be doing so, check egos and insecurities at the door, don't let an outsider cause internal conflict, protect each other, shut down the bullshit from the "simple bitches" (men and women), be a guide for those following behind and, most of all, keep **the code of confidentiality**. This allows them to safely show vulnerability with each other. Vulnerability? Yes, but they do not expose their few weaknesses to "just anyone." The circle is their safety zone, and it is guarded.

Where they gather, they have fun, but never assume business is not being handled at the same time, whether visible to others or not. Their high-maintenance standards can intimidate the pseudo kingpins that approach them. Using body language, they execute business while on leisure, from the slight raise of a brow, to the slight grin, to the soul piercing stare and the cross of their legs. These Alpha Females adhere to the Queenpin Code for there is a significant price to pay for committing an infraction. They are anything but **conventional**.

CHAPTER SEVEN

Exposed and Unleashed

The aura that radiates from and surrounds an Alpha Female creates perceptions of impermeable, fearless excellence with a hint of perfection, steadiness, and leader. Most of them are called "Superwoman," when in actuality they compare to "Wonder Woman." Yes, there is a difference.

Her life is best described by the group Mary Mary in the lyrics of "God in Me."

> *"You see her style you think she nice,*
> *you look at her whip you say the whip tight*
> *You look at her crib you thinkin' she paid*
> *you look at her life you think she's got it made*
> *but everything she got the girl's been given*
> *She calls it a blessing but you call it living*
> *When it comes to money she can be a hero*
> *She writes them checks with a whole lot of zeros..."*

People admire the Alpha Female for her aura and stature; yet, curious questioning falls upon the minds of the masses. "Could she really be all those things? Is she lucky? What does she fear? What is her internal battle? What are her weaknesses?" and so many more. Alpha Females are human; so, their egos, fears, and vulnerabilities vary slightly from Alpha to Alpha. One commonality resides among them:

133

They do not expose their inner selves to the masses. Only special situations and highly respected confidants can unleash their innermost thoughts, feelings, and truths which expose their souls. Take a peek into the exposition of the inner soul of the Alpha Female—at least, to the extent she'll allow…

The Addict

Hidden among Alpha Female nation resides one of their darkest collective secrets: *addiction.* Most of them do not realize they are addicts for a good portion of their lives. Non-recognition of this weakness lends itself to always being top-performers, leading in various aspects of their lives. They are the social conductors, the master influencers, and the seducers to the world around them. (Yes, the world around *them.*)

Everyone has vices and addictions they get hooked on and, seemingly, cannot live without: Shoes, clothes, accessories, sex, alcohol, narcotics, and money are typical types of addictions. But, Alpha Females have one common addiction: *power.* Most people view them as *control freaks,* which is true on many levels. But, there lies a major difference between control and power. *Control* is "*to exercise restraint or direction over; dominate; command.*" *Power* is "*the possession of control or command over others; authority; ascendancy; ability to do or act; capability of doing or accomplishing something.*"

The Alpha Female *is* power, and power looms as the Alpha Female's drug of choice. Her need for the continual "hit" from the power-drug is what drives her existence. Power targets range in her life from career to her business, her social network, friends, family, sexual relationships, and overall environment. She places extreme value on her desire for constant achievement, winning at all costs, and attaining a power 'fix,' so she consistently seeks, arranges, and executes the next set of lofty goals for herself and others. When in a "no-win" situation, which is rare, she resorts to the "breaking even/no losing" option, therefore maintaining a sense of power. Once an area of life no longer provides the next level of high, she finds another supplier.

When not reaching her milestones or goals as she expects, she will exert power over other areas. For example, she'll increase her fitness level, creating a better body. She'll replace or completely write off the men on her dating roster who no longer provide the intellectual and sexual high she craves. She snares the powerful man that challenges her while dangling the guy who is the easy mark, knowing she'll have power over him until *she* decides she no longer needs him for her entertainment. She'll walk into a high-end car dealership and buy off the showroom floor. Although these behaviors seem harsh, she performs with such ease and grace that most are unaware of her underlying struggle.

Losing an inner circle friend or family member to death creates the extreme need for the high, as no one controls death. Alpha Females exert power by taking the personal tragedy and creating positive venues; like establishing a scholarship fund or an endowment in the deceased's name. With any upset of power balance in her life—or loss of the high—the Alpha Female will orchestrate power moves to not only restore the balance, but also to push the limits to gain the next high. She does it through seducing people, places, situations, and transactions. The high is the ultimate seduction for her. It is no different from an alcoholic who craves the next drink or a junkie who craves the next narcotic hit. When is enough finally enough? (Hint: There's never enough.) What happens when the high becomes less potent? What happens when the next-level high becomes scarce?

The Dark Side

"To know your Enemy, you must become your Enemy."

—Sun Tzu teachings from *The Art of War*

What happens when you are your own worst enemy? The cliché of this question passes over the lips of masses as a deeper look into one's self. The quote resonates as even deeper truth for an Alpha Female, exposing her ultimate internal battle.

Her internal battle stems from extremely high expectations for achievement and her definition of success, obtaining unattainable excellence, and the need for the power high. What makes her different from others who show similarities? The set standards, measurements, and rewards are completely internally driven; others, when they look deeper, find that these are more externally driven. No external forces or expectations ever compares to the level she creates internally, nurturing her ego. The internal battle, coupled with the monotonous quest of the high, creates an uncontrolled spiral and depressed state in her life. This is called "crashing."

Combating the depressive state varies slightly between Alphas and depends on their beliefs. The commonality exists in that these women rarely ask for help because of the internal belief to always appear unscathed. Known as the go-to person, finding someone who understands and can help becomes rare. Usually only another Alpha Female can detect the internal injury and possess enough understanding to lend a guiding hand. But, how many "Authentic 8s" can there be per capita?

They offset the "crashing" by doing everything possible to obtain the power high in their environment. Acts range from embracing an Obsessive-Compulsive Disorder appearance in their homes and offices to higher-risk, of "suicidal" behaviors of extreme outdoor activities to exceeding fifty gray-shaded sexual activities, and more. She ensures that everything in her home, car, and office shines and has the appearance of excellence. She becomes agitated with the slightest item out of place or time as she tries to counteract the crashing. She usually feels the crashing coming on and tries to backspin out of it. The backspin consists of finding ways to get the endorphin high of power, or perceived power. She will experiment with cocktails, exercise, travel, prescription medicine, and/or intense sex. Sometimes the combination of two or more solves the issue; other times, it is not enough. She does not rely *heavily* on prescriptions or alcohol as, in her mind, these are known to be something to which mere mortals surrender their control. Instead, her libido goes into overdrive as a substitute.

An Alpha Female will spin the globe and take a flight to where it lands as if going to the grocery store. She'll end up on a tropical island, sometimes secluded, where she becomes uninhabited within her own solitude. She knows she possesses the power and ability to do what she wants, when she wants; so, why not fly around the globe at the drop of a hat?

"Sex is about power," as highlighted in earlier chapters, and this is the Alpha Female's supreme mantra when in crashing mode. Her sexual trysts play out on her terms, with powerful positioning. She asserts the complete dominatrix mode with the partner(s) of her choosing. S&M/bondage, deeper fetishes, and experimentation on her sexual partner allow her to push the limits of boundaries and power, giving her more of a pleasure rush. If she takes a more submissive role, she keeps her power by "playing" the role to gain the high she needs. She may even venture deeper into the world of a sex/swingers' club to create another level of intensity. The ultimate exertion of her power lies within her well-hidden Jekyll/Hyde persona; no outsider would have a clue, for she gives no hints.

The lower the low, the higher the high has to be for her. The symptoms and actions mimic many of those to be disclosed by bi-polar subjects. Those that are wired more narcissistic and sociopathic not only walk that dark side themselves, but have no remorse for devouring others in it, pleasuring every moment.

Compared to her Beta counterparts, the lows have to be much more substantial to scathe her. Once injured, pending the level and number of lows, the Alpha Female either rises from the flames like the Phoenix or completely perishes from the incineration. More often, the Phoenix rises, becoming the truthful legend to which folklore is created, which feeds her ego and provides the ultimate high once again. The flipside leads to suicide as her final, ultimate power move. She exerts power to end "it" her way, ensuring that she exits with the presence and look to which she bore. Even in death, this lady is powerful; she has all of her documents, payments, plans, estate, and insurance policies in order, and those left behind are only to follow her instructions to the letter.

For those tempted to believe, "Ahhh…if I take her power, I can control her or eliminate her…" Let the thought leave your mind as quickly as it entered. What many may perceive as power is one hundred fold for an Alpha Female. The measurement of power, internal to her, contains multiple facets. If there is an attempt to harness it or steal it from her, the wrath unleashed upon offenders is one they certainly regret. She shall adjust only to strengthen—as external conflict strengthens her, not weakens her.

Susceptibility of the Unscathed

Other major questions on the minds of the masses are "What do they fear? What are their vulnerabilities?" Many women (and men) label themselves as Alphas. While many people may exhibit some Alpha-like traits, their exposure to vulnerabilities, insecurities, fears, and egos are easily exposed by others, allowing their "strings and levers" to be pulled at will and manipulated by others. They fear the rules, perceptions, and judgments of others. Alpha Females *are* human; which alludes they have fears, insecurities, and egos. The "Authentic 8s" of the game are unmoved by the majority of the external views. Their egos are not worn on their sleeves nor exposed to predators. The harder-core Alpha Females see through bullshit manipulators while utilizing the situations to use against those offenders. They have no tolerance for those who allow themselves to be exposed, or those who risk putting them in harm's way for that type of simple-minded exposure.

Their vulnerabilities present themselves in their risk of inability. One of their vulnerabilities lies in their **health**. These women live life at high speeds of 10,000 rpm, 24 hours/ 7 days a week; negative health issues not only erode the high internal standard, but slow the pace to where they are no longer able to perform. The health issue creeps forward with aging, too. **Aging** can represent weakness in their views because of the perception of slowing down and actually being mortal. The mortality reality is a fear factor for "Wonder Woman."

Although they know logically they are human, their abilities and strengths allow the masses to view them as superheroes, creating the sense of immortality. In addition, losing someone close to them in friendship and age to a terminally ill disease (e.g., to cancer) or instantly and unexpectedly (e.g., in an accident) creates the huge fear of mortality. The fear resonates not in dying itself as much as to the tick-tock against their plans, goals, and accomplishments. Alpha Females respect the permanent power of death as it trumps *their* power every time. Being sidelined due to health issues for an Alpha Female tortures her spirit. She compensates in other ways to utilize the time, but when it comes to the deeper issues, those that could be terminal, it creates a nagging fear.

These women fear nothing yet fear everything. How could that be? These ladies are the risk takers, the heavy hitters, and the headstrong to what crosses their paths. Everything they fear starts with them exhibiting the ability to live up to their own expectations. The expectations of others have minimal, if any, effect on Alpha Females, as their expectations of themselves always outweigh those of others. They do fear their secrets, vulnerabilities, and insecurities being exposed to the masses. They fear permanent loss of *power*. Power imbalances bring about the lows and crashing to which she finds ways to align back into balance. The possibility of the inability to regain and maintain overall power remains in the back of their psyches.

A question arises from people, even those that consider themselves Alpha: "What happens when an Alpha Female is among other Alphas, does she remain Alpha?" Anyone who considers themselves Alpha and poses this question solidifies the fact they are not a true Alpha. True Alphas never pose this question; they already know the answer. True Alpha Females have no fear of others; in reality they share a mutual respect of each other in person and space. An Alpha Female among other Alphas whom she does not know feels right at home. They will compete for the same goal, but with respect for each other and with a "let the best woman win" mentality. Even if one has a moment of animosity, she never exposes it; she knows the Alpha code of "no simple bitch shit." Honor another Alpha Female as you expect to be honored.

Unleashed

"By looking in the mirror of others,
we come to see the reflection of ourselves."

—Christine Hannon, fitness expert,
world traveler, author

For the Alpha Female, this quote enables her to be unleashed. She looks in the mirror of the masses and compares it to the mirror of other Alphas. The maturity of the Alpha Female grows within; allowing her to transcend from questioning herself to growing into knowing herself; then harnessing the power within to break the confines of those trying to control her.

Regardless of her nationality, religion, heritage, skin tone, height, weight, age, an Alpha Female is who she is. *She is truly born, not made.* They are the "Authentic 8s," possessing all that the number eight represents: personal power, authority, confidence, executive, ego, truth and integrity, and more. Biblically, it represents a new beginning or resurrection, which applies as she continues to resurrect herself from the flames that engulf her. Do not mistake the perception that Augmented Alphas, or betas, are perceived of being valued as any less of a person. The acknowledged communication is the Authentic Alpha Female is wired very differently than most females.

There is an X-factor gene, "AMtrogen-8," that creates the Alpha Female within society, within families, and within siblings. The "AMtrogen-8" mutation continues to elude the pinpointing of the precise combination of DNA responsible for creating it. Although clearly recognized the mutation formula exists, and creates consistent distinctive patterns of thinking, movements, characteristics, behaviors, and desires, the mutation remains a mystery. It's hard to "put a finger on it," yet one knows it when they see it.

An unleashed Alpha Female in the corporate world becomes a talented force, when leveraged properly, creating astronomical positive business returns for any employer. She seduces the environment around her to leverage gains for herself. She is the "Queen Bitch" among bitches ("bitches," in this case, includes bitchy men) as she stands her ground, knows her own mind, allows herself to be political to a point, and nips the bullshit in the bud. There comes a time in her life and career when she may not realize that the game she believes she is playing is actually playing her, and that getting what she wants "at all costs" can come with a hefty price tag. These two points weigh heavily in where her ego lies.

Most true Alphas can control their egos as to not expose their Achilles heel. However, some carry Humpty Dumpty-eggshell egos which create a "pseudo Alpha" perception. The eggshell ego is the one that gets exposed easily by both men and women and, if not careful, it lets the game play them corporately and socially as they are fed what they want to hear and given the view they want to see. It becomes the strings and levers that controls them rather than them being the chess master or puppeteer.

Many true Alphas wear "getting what they want at all costs" as a badge of honor. Tenacity is the badge; but, what happens when it comes at a "price" they were not expecting? The price is the premium they put at risk to lose. Do they notice the value of the risk or is the ego such that it blinds them to it? The value can come in the form of their health, platonic friendships, intimate relationships, corporate relationships, money, and other assets. If the Alpha Female does not value those things in relation to her own goals, then it is easy for her to dismiss them and the blow back will be left in the wake. However, if she does value it in any way, and does not comes to terms to adjust, she risks losing it— never to regain it at the level she originally had it. This loss happens especially when the relationships are with other Alphas, hence the Alpha code.

Men, pay attention. When it comes to dating Alpha Females, excellence is a requirement, not an option. From the initial approach, keep in mind they are not going to respond positively (if at all) to the "one size fits all" lines used on most women. They are not snobs, but are easily turned off. They prefer the genuine to the pretentious, as they see through the bullshit easily and will either dismiss you quickly or entertain you just enough to entertain themselves—until they are no longer amused. They welcome men approaching them as they are not frigid or cold, but the man has to be secure in his approach, not arrogant, pushy, selfish, or self-entitled. No man is "God's gift to her."

If you ace the introduction, propose a date and she accepts, be mindful of how to approach her on the first date. Most men believe they know, but while interviewing many for this book, it was evident many were not in the ballpark of understanding. The date can either be simple or elaborate, but no clichés. If the date is not going well, don't be surprised if she pays for the evening to let you know she can afford not to be bothered any longer and owes you nothing. She'll be impressed more with the man paying attention to her enough in their conversations to be intuitive on what makes the great first date. She's a queen and expects royalty treatment. It is not about the cost, although a cheap man need not apply. It is about the regality. If you don't bring your "A" game, it's over.

An Alpha Female usually matches better with Alpha Males. If a Beta Male makes it to dating status, he must be an extremely secure Beta Male with heavy Alpha-like tendencies. One of the main dating challenges for an Alpha Female is the "love to hate" issue. The qualities and characteristics drawing men to her can also bring her partners to resent her; many times due to men believing they will control, possess, or change her—which is a false belief. Sometimes this woman finds herself in dangerous, stalker-type situation after the man "loving them with disdain" is rejected. The stalking can take place personally and professionally. As for marriage, it's not a top priority. She prefers an engagement or an unlabeled committed relationship to maintain freedom.

Sexual libidos for an Alpha Female mimic that of a man, many times being higher. She has no hard and fast rules about sex; it is more on how she feels and what she wants, when she wants it. If she decides to have a one-night stand, she does so without regret or drama. She is not a whore, but does not conform to society's definition of a "good girl." She knows what she enjoys and is not afraid to ensure she is satisfied.

This woman is more than in control: she harnesses the sexual energy and control as power. Can she be submissive in the bedroom? Sure. But it's an illusion to gain the pleasure she seeks; she maintains the power status throughout. She is the puppet master, pulling the strings to men's mind, body, and souls and using them at will in various situations.

One of the most fascinating observations of her persona in the bedroom is her "Dr. Jekyll /Ms. Hyde" personality, as if leading a double-life. It is said that "Every man wants a lady in the streets and a freak in the sheets." Her persona dignifies her to a classier level than the cliché statement. There's no hint to her lack of sexual inhibition and freedom she possesses, as it is well-hidden and separate from the professional branding she owns. Even the most edge-pushing levels of sexual adventures are still executed with class and style. She wants a man that can take control; if he does not or cannot, he is dismissed from the roster. She does not "fake it," as this would be a complete waste of her energy and time. Why bother? She will let him know if he does not live up to her challenge, and will either cut the night short or bring things to an abrupt stop and walk away.

She takes pride in controlling the pleasure of her partner for she knows the psychological control it provides over him. At the same time, it is all about her (although she can make him feel that it's all about him). She has her own fantasies, fetishes, and erotic hot spots. The men who tap into them discover themselves embarking into unchartered territories of pleasure. She may belong to elite clubs that are nowhere near her residence. She promotes no evidence and extreme confidentiality. Sex is a weapon; and, in some cases sex-with-an-agenda becomes a theme. Men can be romantic, but overly sappy men will turn her off immediately. She's definitely into foreplay which becomes an event within itself. An Alpha Female's eroticisms vary depending on the woman, usually far exceeding those of most women and many men.

Men who engage with them must be discreet. They cannot be ready to tell all—not over cocktails, on social media, nowhere. Men who are instigators or spread rumors are not tolerated. An Alpha Female will scope them to identify if those qualities exist; if found, they may become a good acquaintance, but they will not enter the inner sanctum and sex is definitely not an option. She may not explicitly inform them of their status; if arrogant or egotistically pushy, she may influence his movements without him being aware. A true Alpha Male is the only person to which she will "submit," especially in the bedroom. This lady sets the tone from which legends are created.

An Alpha Female has no desire to be labeled or treated as the "perceived average woman" or what society believes a woman's lot in life contains. If she decides to marry, she's selective and takes her time. Many prefer not to be "leashed" to another person officially. She can be engaged and committed in a relationship, but marriage does not interest most. An Alpha Female likes children; if she decides to have offspring, it is usually one. She understands the demand of children and the "leashing" of duties that could interfere with her goals and life plans. She wants the power to choose to do what she wants, when she wants, without having to answer to anyone. Marriage and children can erode that power.

She is the powerful "mob boss" who leads and protect her family, trusted circle of friends, and overall environment. She usually travels in packs of three or four. She knows and is expected to adhere to the unwritten honor/trust code of Alphas. Her stealthy movements mimic those of the exotic panther. Whether in a restaurant or on a vacation, this lady is poetry in motion; her aura causes others to give her the "red carpet" treatment. When you see a group of them, make no mistake, they are having fun; but, "the family" business discussions are taking place. They know their individual and combined power and they don't hesitate to flex it.

That power, individually and collectively, is the Alpha Female's number one drug. Power gives her an insatiable high she cannot resist. The drug high comes in various forms and she keeps the continual high flowing. Her addiction stays tucked away with her other secrets. As with any humans, she has fears and insecurities; however, an Alpha Female does not wear them on her sleeve, but keeps them under lock and key only to be revealed to her inner circle, if even to them. It usually takes another Alpha to notice and relate. These ladies harness the power to appear unscathed, untouchable, and unleashed. She dominates with power, beauty, and soul.

If no other awakening opportunity is gained from this book, the most important unleashing event of society is accepting the Alpha Female as the new, normal "bar" for women. She does not follow conventional female societal roles and will never hang her head in shame. Ladies who may not want to marry, have children, or adhere to the "submissive laws" of society and religion can hold their heads high, stand in purpose, and know that the shackles no longer bind. She is the epitome of "Beauty, Power, and Soul."

Unleashing Your Inner Alpha

"Do I have inner Alpha Female traits?"
"How do I use them?"

Many women have snippets of various Alpha traits that help them navigate successfully. Many worry about the social stigmas of displaying those traits; however, the first step to unleashing your inner Alpha is to recognize it and embrace it for yourself. Once you begin to embrace your inner Alpha traits, you can embark on your true journey.

This book brings awareness to Alpha Females and peeks into their inner beings, traits, and movements. Stay tuned for the next segment, *Unleashing the Alpha Within You,* to discover how to utilize *your* inner Alpha.